Sister Savior

Sister Savior

*A Story of Collective Liberation
through Sisterhood*

BRITTANIE RICHARDSON

RESOURCE *Publications* · Eugene, Oregon

SISTER SAVIOR
A Story of Collective Liberation through Sisterhood

Resource Publications
An Imprint of Wipf and Stock Publishers
199 W. 8th Ave., Suite 3
Eugene, OR 97401

www.wipfandstock.com

PAPERBACK ISBN: 978-1-6667-8574-6
HARDCOVER ISBN: 978-1-6667-8575-3
EBOOK ISBN: 978-1-6667-8576-0

VERSION NUMBER 11/01/23

For more information, address: brittaniemrichardson@gmail.com

Content Warning: *Sister Savior* is a contemporary memoir and includes graphic descriptions of sexual abuse of a minor.

To Tiffanie and Mommie
Thank you for saving me

To my daughters, the original chicakadoos—
Amina (big), Sarah, Amina (small), and Faith

Thank you for saving each other

Contents

Acknowledgments

THIS BOOK IS NOT MINE, it's ours. It would not exist without the incredible people and communities that have held me up through the years and got me to the point of writing this book and beyond. I can't name you all here, but you know who you are. Thank you for being a part of me and a part of my story. I love you and deeply appreciate you.

To my devoted parents Brian and Sharon, and the whole Richardson and Bullard families, thank you for loving me, raising me and accepting me for exactly who I am. Because of your nurturing and support I am able to tell my story. I am able to take the pain in my life and turn it into medicine and healing for myself and the world because I know that I always have you guys back home in my corner. I honor you.

To my godmother and auntie Angela—thank you for all of your spiritual direction on my path. You have been the voice of the Holy Spirit for me on my journey.

Gram and Grandma, thank you for all your prayers for me. They are coming true.

To my friends—you mean the world to me. All of you, all over the world. Thank you for accepting me as part of you. Your support gives me so much strength. I love you back.

To Natasha, Danielle and Laurita, your friendship in our formative years and beyond has shaped me in ways you'll never know. You will always have a special place in my heart. I love you my bests.

Ellie, there are no words. This book wouldn't exist without you and neither would I. I love you as much as I can love a person. I also want to thank you, my dear friend Mukami, my therapist Najia, and all of the people in Kenya who have been a part of literally keeping me alive over the years. Thank you guys for always reminding me that my life has worth and putting in the energy to help sustain it, even when my illness tries to kill me. I love you all.

Denise Vazquez Troutman, decades ago challenged me to stop living small and saying no to life's invitations to more by saying to me, "If you're invited somewhere, even to the grocery store, go!" I have been going ever since. To places much more adventurous than the grocery store. It has changed the course of my life.

Thank you Chuck Alphin for taking me on my first trip to the continent where it all started.

To my teachers at Pebblebrook High School and University of the Arts, also to Freddie Hendricks, Charles Bullock, and all of YEA, thank you for nurturing me as an artist.

To Anthony DeMauro, Bela Shah, and Dalai Lama Fellows 2020 Cohort, thank you for being incredible community to me as I experienced and wrote this book. You're amazing!

Mary Lugano, Anita Ntale and Michelle Angweni ("The Ancestors" lol)—thank you for being midwives to both this book and my life in Kilifi. I'll always remember celebrating the completion of the manuscript on the dhow with you guys. Thank you for seeing me.

Chris and Jenn Hadsell, thank you for loving and holding me and the girls before, during and after the transition from the home in Kenya. Thank you for seeing the good in me.

To the churches that have sustained the girls and I and nurtured us in numerous ways: Community Fellowship Baptist Church, New Life Christian Center, The Way Berkeley, Central Avenue Church, The Proverbial Experience and Sensual Faith Sundays, thank you for being exactly who you say you are —the church. I couldn't do this work without you.

To all of the people who supported Art and Abolition in all the ways you did from the beginning to end, thank you so much. Together, we did exactly what we set out to do! You are world changers!

To the one and only Stella Ninah-Buluma herself, thank you for taking this journey with me and doing it with such grace and love. To those who transitioned to Circle of Care Kenya with me and continue to support me and the girls, I appreciate you.

Rozz Nash, Natalie Carter, Poorni Bid, and Lyvonne Briggs, you have been unwavering in your consistent presence and support of both me and the girls. Your partnership means the world to me. You keep me going. I love you.

To Nyaya, Mama Sarah, Mama Amina and all the biological mamas and family members of our girls who have also become friends of mine and beloved co-parents, I honor you and am eternally grateful for your partnership in the greatest journey of my life. Tukopamoja wamama. Nawapenda sana.

Girls (all of you), I love you with my whole heart. Thank you for being more than my daughters, but for also being great spiritual teachers in my life.

Louis Greenstein, thank you for making me feel like a real writer and for the work you did on this book. You and Catherine are so precious to me.

Liz, Baby, thank you for choosing me. I can't wait to continue this story by creating many more joyous chapters with you by my side.

Harriet Tubman, I honor you.

To God, my Beloved, you are so good and so faithful. Thank you for always bringing me back to You. Thank you for working everything out for my good.

CHAPTER 1

Baby Girl

PRAYER

Growing up, God was real to me. As real as the sun that rose and set every day. It was that easy. That sure. God just was. I had a lot of imaginary friends, but God was my favorite. I can't remember the moment I fell in love with God. I just remember loving. I just remember being, as if we always were. I was brought up in the Christian faith, so Jesus was my God and I loved Him. He was my best friend. I would talk to Jesus all the time about everything. Prayer was like God: easy. I would pray while walking home from school with the sun shining on my face, or in church on my knees with my eyes tightly closed and my hands pressed against each other. I would pray before every meal and before falling asleep at night.

I also prayed in the hard times when it was dark. I believe that I prayed even way back when. In a time only my body, soul and spirit remember. Way back when I decided to leave the other realm and come to this one. Prematurely according to this world, through a young, Black, under-resourced mother. Early and underdeveloped, but also right on time. My organs were not quite done forming yet, specifically my heart and my lungs. Even as I write this decades later, my body still remembers "way back when," transitioning into this world where hearts are supposed to beat, and lungs are supposed to breathe. But mine were premature. They didn't fully do that yet. So I arrived on this side with a broken heart and gasping for breath. I arrived screaming and flailing with stolen breaths. No words yet. *"I can't breathe,"* I said. I prayed to God even then.

LUNGS AND HEART

I have a memory of being maybe four years old or so, I don't really know what age, but I was very young. So I use my imagination mixed with my memory and come up with the closest things to the truth I can. So let's say I was about four. At the time I was living with Bill and Judy, who I thought were my parents. But I later learned that they were not my biological parents. They never were legally fostering me. I have never been in the foster care system. But this couple raised me for the first few years of my life in their home to help my incredible biological mother that truly did the best she could when she could. That's part of why I was so confused and upset when Judy told me one day that both her and my real mommy were my mommies, and she promised to always love me and always parent me too. I didn't know then she was doing that thing that adults do when we aren't brave enough to tell children the truth of what's happening, to break their hearts. Even if their hearts are already broken. We forget that heartbreak is a part of life and something kids can live through. Whose heartbreak are we really protecting them from? Theirs? Our own? What Judy was avoiding saying was "shit is about to hit the fan."

Painfully, in an effort to keep me safe, I was later taken away from Judy and Bill and went to live with my biological mother, "Mommie." Mommie was hurt, shocked and livid when I told her that her friends Judy and Bill told me they were my parents. She assured me that she was my mother. It was confusing for me as a small child. Even after I moved out of Judy and Bill's place, thankfully, Mommie allowed Judy to continue babysitting me. I told Judy what happened when she was babysitting me one day. She pulled me up on her lap and wiped my tears. She told me "I am still your mommy. Don't cry. I'll always be here for you. We are just going to play a game. When your mom is around, call me 'Judy,' but any other time you can call me 'Mommy.' It's a game we are going to play, okay?" I stopped crying, smiled and said "okay." It didn't sound like grooming then, it sounded like safety. I thought I was safe. I thought there was enough love to go around, and I could have both my mothers. I thought she was telling me the truth.

But whose heart was she actually attempting to protect? Hers or mine? Mine was already broken. She knew this. And what was she afraid of? Taking my breath away? At that time breath was fleeting for me. A novel commodity I adored but could not always access. I have memories of losing my breath often. When I finally learned to speak I remember communicating to the adults in my life, "I can't breathe." This was followed by ambulance rides and hospital visits. Brown paper bags over my mouth as I hyperventilated. Was this simply a medical issue? Or did I know? Did my body know? Was my body telling me, "Something bad is going to happen. Something bad has happened. Mommie, something bad is happening"?

DADDY IN THE DARK

The night that it happened, Bill, the man I called "Daddy," woke me from my sleep in the middle of the night. He told me to go to the bathroom so I would not wet the bed as I normally did. I woke up and rubbed my sleepy eyes with my small hands and innocently told Daddy that I didn't have to pee. I was wearing a white nightgown with pink frills at the bottom and Bugs Bunny on the front. I couldn't have been more than a few feet tall. He was big and I was small. He got very angry and took off his belt and snapped it, then barked at me to go to the bathroom. I was afraid, but not surprised by his behavior. He was a violent, alcoholic man. But this was the first time that I was having an experience like what was to come that night. Until then, I didn't know that nightmares could happen when you were awake. I slowly walked to the bathroom. The pink frills of my nightgown brushed against my small brown calves with each step. Daddy walked in front of me, leading the way.

We entered the bathroom.

He left the door wide open.

Weirdly, he closed the lid of the toilet and sat down on top of it. How was I supposed to pee like he had told me to if the toilet was closed and he was sitting on it? Oh well, I was too sleepy to think too deeply about it. I rubbed my eyes again.

This memory is a bit blurry, maybe because I want it to be, maybe because it was so long ago, maybe because of the gaslighting that happened afterward. But this is the first time I remember my "daddy" groping my non-existent breasts from behind as he pulled my body toward him with his legs wide open, and then using his rough hands and large fingers to rub and touch my smooth, prepubescent vagina. He forcefully turned me around to face him and then pulled me toward him again. He forced his tongue into my mouth repeatedly which I didn't understand, and thought was very strange. I didn't even know at the time that this was "kissing." The only kind of kissing I knew about had nothing to do with tongues or force. The kisses I knew and missed in that moment were soft and landed

3

on cheeks or foreheads or lips with care and then quickly flew away. But in that dark bathroom with the door wide open he whispered in his husky grown up voice "kiss me." And when I went in to give him our usual innocent peck, he forced his tongue into my mouth and down my throat. It was hard and messy, and it did not fly away. I was confused. Mouths were for pecking, not for plunging. Like chests were for gripping when gasping for air, not for groping.

This went on for what seemed like forever. It was confusing. I felt deeply sad that this was happening, but I wasn't sure why. I didn't know that daddies weren't supposed to do this to their little girls. I definitely didn't know that it was an act of violence. I just didn't like it.

He sat on the toilet panting like a dog and rubbing my vagina as he held me in front of him with my nightgown pulled up around my waist. The rubbing hurt. The fact that it hurt made it even more confusing because as he was rubbing he kept asking, "Does it feel good?" Somehow, I knew that I was supposed to say yes, even though it felt like his hands were slicing me down there. As an adult I look back and guess that he was looking for my clitoris. I guess that's what he was intending to rub. But all I remember is the more he rubbed, the more pain I felt and eventually even though I kept answering "yes" to his breathy "Baby, does that feel good to you?" I couldn't hold my pain in anymore. It started to spill out of my eyes through hot salty tears pouring down my cheeks. He eventually saw my tears and responded by telling me that there is no reason to cry. Is that when I learned not to trust my own tears? He asked me why I was crying. I said, "I just want to go to my room and play with my dolls." I somehow knew that I wasn't supposed to tell the rest of the truth, that I wasn't supposed to tell him that in that moment my love and admiration for him as my daddy was turning into a hot hate—a hate that would eventually turn to rage and spew onto people who made me feel vulnerable. At that moment I felt myself close. There in the bathroom, door wide open, being digitally raped by my "daddy," I prayed the most sincere prayer that I knew how to pray. My little three or four-year-old self begged God quietly, trying to hide my tears, "Please God, make it stop."

He didn't.

God as I knew him, the white grandpa-like God in the sky, never showed up. But minutes later, my sister did. My beautiful Black girl sister. In that moment, my savior was a little Black girl, just like me.

4

As Bill was switching back and forth between forcing his tongue in my mouth, telling me never to tell anyone and rubbing my vagina, my sister showed up at the door of the bathroom. I was so happy he had left the door wide open. She looked at Bill on the toilet, pants undone, and me standing in front of him, nightgown raised. Shame overcame me. But something stronger than shame lifted my head, and I locked eyes with my sister, my savior. Then I knew. I knew that because my sister was there at that door, I could pull my nightgown down and stop crying. I knew that because my sister was there the violence would stop. It was then that I knew what kind of savior I wanted. What kind of God I wanted. I didn't want the white grandpa God in the sky. I wanted my God to be like my sister: to show up and make violence stop.

In the years that followed, my understanding of what a savior was—which came directly from that very personal and lived experience with my sister—was stolen from me. Before I knew it, saviors weren't sisters. In fact saviors didn't even look like them. Apparently my experience was wrong and in time I came to learn that the Bible was right.

I began going to church where I learned that there was an Ultimate Savior, a savior of all of humanity. But surprisingly, this savior was actually male and according to the kiddie bibles with animated pictures that I read, he was also white. As I grew up I would continue to learn about this Jesus figure that I had been introduced to and told to worship. This Jesus had some values. Back then I understood these values in my child brain to be things like "be good" and "obey your parents." They started out innocently enough. Like religion tends to. But as I continued to drink the Kool-Aid I began to ingest the stuff that made the Kool-Aid good. The white stuff, the sugar that makes you want to keep drinking. And that "stuff" was white supremacy, racism, colorism, patriarchy, misogyny, queer phobia and the list goes on. These systems I was drinking in would rape me, wound me, make me hate myself, gaslight me, and silence me just like my "daddy" did for years and years to come. This toxic theology is where I learned to devalue my "girlness."

Men were saviors.

Girls were virgins.

The end.

It erased my belief in the power I inherently had as a girl, as a Black girl, and convinced me that I was powerless. It taught me the message that I was a dark-skinned, dirty, ugly little Black girl who needed to be saved by a man who was white and pure and perfect and beautiful and had all the power. I believed this message. I believed that white Jesus with His heart full of light could rescue me. Save me. Make my darkness go away. I wanted so desperately for my darkness to go away. I wanted his beauty to make my ugly go away. For his clean to make my dirty go away.

It didn't. He didn't. White Jesus never saved me. My black ass sister did.

BEDSHEETS

The moment in the bathroom is the most vivid memory I have of heart-break coming from the outside instead of the inside. But there are also other experiences around sexual and physical abuse that stick out and contribute to the shattering. Little pieces falling off along the way. I left traces of pieces of my heart everywhere I walked around that apartment. But apparently, the only one who could see them was me. Although I had my own bedroom and my own bed, I slept between Judy and Bill in their bed at night for much of the time I lived with them. My brain chooses not to remember what happened on those nights, lying between them.

I do remember our daily routine of waking up to sheets soaked with my urine. I was too old to be wetting the bed by then so I would be pun-ished for it every morning. Our routine went something like this: wake up to wet bed sheets, be scolded by Mommy or Daddy, get into the bathtub with my toys and play until one of them came to wash my body, and then when it was the end of bath time, whoever was bathing me would ask me to stand up. They would look me in my eyes and ask if I was ready for my spanking. Every morning, I bowed my head and said yes. They would then fold the leather belt in their hand and spank my wet butt with it several times. Each hit would make a splattering sound. The hits were also quite hard, so it was difficult for me to remain standing in the slippery bathtub. They would grasp my arm really tight as they hit me to keep me from slip-ping. I never cried. I felt I deserved this. When Mommy did it, she would always hug me and tell me she loved me afterward. Each time I would make up my mind not to wet the bed ever again. But then the following morning would be the same: wet sheets, bath, spanking, guilt, hug, "I'll never do it again." I wet the bed until I was sixteen years old.

BAD DREAM

If Bill broke my heart from the outside for the first time, it was Judy who broke it second. I would like to say that the sexual abuse happened behind Judy's back, but I have to admit, she knew. If she didn't know from her intuition, she definitely knew when I told her.

One day when Bill was working in his basement workshop and Judy and I were hanging out in their bedroom together, I somehow got up the courage to tell her. I had recently seen a puppet show at school that taught us about good places to be touched by adults and bad places to be touched by adults. Watching that puppet show was the first time I realized that what was happening to me was bad, what Daddy was doing to me was very, very bad. As the play went on and on for what seemed like forever, I remember feeling shame. It stuck to me like glue. And I felt like everyone could see the shame on me, that everyone knew what was happening to me. It wasn't and Daddy's and my secret anymore. At the end of the play the performers told us that if anything like this was happening to us we needed to tell an adult we trusted immediately. That's when I knew I had to tell my Mommy. We were in their bedroom. I was sitting on the bed. I began to muster up the courage to tell her about what Daddy was doing to me in the bathroom and how the people at school said it was bad. I took a breath and right as I was about to confess I saw the leather belt hanging from the closet door. I exhaled and stayed quiet for a bit. A couple of minutes later as she was standing by the window I burst out, "Mommy, I have to tell you something, but promise you won't tell Daddy."

Judy replied, "Okay baby, I promise."

I inhaled again and then the words just fell out of my mouth. "Daddy raped me."

"*What?*" she replied.

I said it again, this time with a little more firmness. "Daddy raped me."

She said nothing. Her face remained white and blank. She took me by the arm and led me exactly where I told her not to: to Daddy's workshop. She told me to sit. They went in the back and talked. That workshop was another one of Bill's favorite places to fondle me. He would teach me about his tools, one hand on my nonexistent breast and one down his pants.

A couple of moments later Judy and Bill came to where I was sitting. Bill was smiling. Judy was not. Bill sat me on his lap and looked me in my eyes. He asked, "What did you tell Mommy?"

I was so scared. "You raped me," I said. The words no longer felt awkward in my mouth. But they tasted sour.

He laughed softly; a smile pasted to his face in response to me. "No, no, no Bree. That never happened. You must have had a bad dream. Daddy would never do something like that to you. Daddy loves you."

Then Judy chimed in "See, Bree? It was just a dream. A bad dream. Okay?" I bowed my head, the same way I did in preparation for my spankings in the bathtub. "Okay," I replied, knowing this was a lie.

"Repeat after me," Judy said, "It was only a dream."

I held back my tears and repeated, "It was only a dream." Bill laughed slyly at the sound of this.

Judy popped up from her seat and smiled. "Now if you promise not to say anything like that again, we can go to Chuck E. Cheese today!" I looked up at my smiling parents, swallowed my voice and my pain. I promised myself I would never try to tell the truth about my pain ever again.

I don't remember if we actually went to Chuck E. Cheese that day or not.

The digital rape, molestation—whatever term I was using at the time—remained my secret until it came pouring out of me almost accidentally years later to an adult who believed me. Again, I felt so much guilt and shame afterward. I also felt like I was being punished. Because of my confession, I was never allowed to go to Bill and Judy's house again. Mommie wouldn't allow it. This was my third major outside-of-my-body heartbreak. She was trying to keep me safe. As an adult I know that my mother was protecting me from a violent predator. But at the time, it felt like I was being ripped apart from the first mother I ever remembered knowing.

ANGER

I have a vague memory of the day I was taken away from Judy and Bill's house to go live with Mommie. I remember early in the day Judy gently trying to explain to me what was going to happen. I remember evening coming. I'm not actually sure if it was evening but in my memory it is dark for one reason or another. People showed up at our door. I don't remember who. I remember hiding behind a huge recliner, not wanting to be snatched away from Judy, who I innocently loved more than anyone in the world, from the only home I had ever known, from what I felt to be love. I was afraid. Eventually some adult scooped me up in their big arms and began carrying me out the door away from Judy. The trek from behind the chair to the door was long and painful. In reality, I'm not sure if I was screaming with my mouth or just in my heart. I am not sure if tears were actually streaming down my cheeks and my arms were actually flailing the way I remember them to be, or if I lay limp in the person's arms as they carried me away and I actually had my tantrum on the inside. Had I begun hiding my pain yet? But whether it happened outwardly or inwardly, as I was carried along that long journey, I kicked and I screamed and I wailed and I protested. I looked Judy in the eyes and yelled, "Mommy! Mommy! No!" I tried to escape from this person's big arms. I tried to remove the widening distance between me and my life as I knew it, between me and a weeping red-faced Judy. I tried to make her love me enough to tell them to stop and for her to sweep me up in her arms and wipe my tears and tell me it's okay and that she's sorry and that it's over now. But the distance just kept getting wider. Before I knew it we were closer to the door than the chair. I screamed, flailed, begged for my life, for my love. Judy stood in the same spot and let the distance widen. She let them take me away. She didn't protect me. She didn't change her mind when we got to the door. She didn't run toward me and rescue me out of this person's arms. She watched me go. She stood there and watched. As the years went by the pain from this experience turned to anger and eventually to rage.

BROKEN PROMISES

I never saw Judy again. We talked on the phone I think three times during my adolescence. The first two times she made promises that she didn't keep. Once, around Christmastime, she promised to come meet me in a park in Chicago after years of separation. She never showed up. The second time she called, I was living in Georgia, and I was visiting my dad's house when I picked up my cell phone and it was her. She promised to send me some special trinkets from my childhood and told me how much she and Daddy missed me and how often they looked through my pictures and talked about me. Why did she have to bring him up? It hurt me when she referenced him. I have always felt that she chose him over me, which she did. That crushed me. I was her daughter. I wanted to be chosen. I wanted to be believed. I wanted to be rescued by her. I wanted her to come and scoop me up and place my head against her chest and let me wail as she stroked my hair and told me, "it's okay." I wanted her to be a mommy to me again. I had a deep painful gnawing need for presence, love and affection. The painful need sat deep in my chest. That need never got fulfilled. She never came for me. She never apologized. She never held me against her chest. She was never my mommy again. I felt like a newborn baby—abandoned, screaming for my mother, needing to be nursed at her breast. And she never came. She neglected me. She rejected me. That shit pissed me off. And it stayed with me. I became a screamer. My deep sadness turned into a red-hot rage. I became fucking angry.

The third and final time she called me was the day of my Auntie's wedding. My sisters and I were junior bridesmaids. We were all at the salon getting our hair done when she called. She called to tell me that she was going into surgery and wasn't sure if she would make it out alive. That's all I remember from the conversation. I have never heard from her since.

CHAPTER 2

Big Girl

BEING TAKEN AWAY FROM Judy felt like a loss, but little did I know I was being rescued by my true mother and carried into a cradle of care that was real and loving and non-violent. A big part of this cradle of care was my grandmothers who have now passed. One of the great mothers in my life, the matriarch in our family who helped raise my sister Tiffanie and me, was my great grandmother, "Gram."

Gram died when I was young, less than thirteen years old, but her impact on my life is massive. I have followed in her legacy in many ways. I remember spending lots of days with her in the senior citizen's home where she lived. She had a small one-bedroom apartment; my sister and I would often stay there when Mommie was at work. I remember spending entire days just playing cards with Gram. Her favorite card game was called Kings Corner. I don't know if that's a real game or if the old folks made it up. But I remember her forcing us to play it with her on her rickety portable tray in her living room, and even in the bathroom as she sat on the toilet. We would also spend several hours per day in the day room downstairs with the other old folks playing Kings Corner and drinking lots of Mountain Dew. There were vending machines in the day room which was the most amazing thing to Tiffanie and me as kids. Going to the vending machine was one of the highlights of our days at the senior citizens home with Gram. Gram's was nothing like Judy's. Had I found another model for what my savior is like?

After work, Mommie would pick us up in the evening and as she got us ready to go, I remember Gram always nagging her about getting us baptized. We were young and in Catholic school. But even still, I didn't understand what the big deal was about baptism. To Gram, it was a big fucking deal. So big that it warranted being talked about every single day. I remember the day that I actually got baptized. It was in the Catholic church, and I was wearing white. Unfortunately Gram had already died by then. But a couple years before she died, she said something to me that has stuck with me until this day. I was maybe eleven years old when it happened. I had just finished cooking her breakfast and was serving it to her on an ironing board because we were at Mom's house so we didn't have the rickety little tray she normally ate on. Gram was very thin by this time and her mouth was full of only gums. Her gray hair was pulled back with a black hair clamp, and as I placed her plate before her she gently held my arm, looked me straight in the eye and said, "You are special. There is something different about you. You are going to do great things with your life." She smiled at the thought of my future and then looked down and concentrated on eating her breakfast. My heart felt like it was on fire after hearing those words. I vowed to make them a reality.

At the end of her life Gram got really sick and could no longer be a caregiver. She had to be cared for. Her daughter—my grandmother whom the whole family lovingly calls "Mom"—moved her into her home and became Gram's caregiver.

The first time I ever saw a dead body was when we all went to go to see Gram before she was cremated. I thought it would make me really sad and be really scary. But I don't remember being afraid at all. I still remember what her lifeless body looked like, especially her face. It looked like her except without her in it. I remember crying, but I am not sure if I was crying for myself or if I was crying for the people around me. Especially Mom, who was completely devastated at the loss of her mother.

As a child, I remember life before Gram, and life after Gram. Life before Gram was holidays at Mom's house with a huge spread of food covering the table. Me, Tiffanie, Mommie, Mom, Uncie (my uncle), Auntie (my maternal aunt), and Gram would all gather for the holidays. On Thanksgiving there was sometimes space made on the table for Gram's birthday cake. My most holy moments have been with my grandparents around dining room tables. Life before Gram was family and laughter and jokes and hugs and kisses. Life after Gram felt almost like an apology. It felt like the whole family was kind of apologizing for existing without her, or maybe existing as a form of resistance to living without her.

I remember when Mom brought Gram's ashes home and put them up on the mantle. Having her ashes there made Gram feel closer. It made me feel safe. I remember Mom would always put a bottle of Mountain Dew next to her urn. As a child I believed that the amount of Mountain Dew would reduce overnight. I totally believed Gram was drinking it. How could ashes drink Mountain Dew? I didn't question that. Gram had already joined Tiffanie and Mommie in the league of saviors in my life, even to the point of divinity. So of course she could drink Mountain Dew even when dead! I believed these women could do anything. They were pieces of God after all.

GRANDMA

My paternal grandmother's name was Juanita Bullard. She died when I was in college. My last memory of her is lying in bed with her as she was very frail and sick. I was showing her pictures from my study abroad trip to South Africa. She was so proud of me. Grandma was a fiery Christian prayer warrior. She's probably the reason I ever became a Christian in the first place and her prayers are probably what brought me back to my faith after I broke up with it for a while. I fully believe that her prayers are still working in my life right now. My memories of spending summers at her and my grandfather's two-bedroom apartment in Indiana are filled with waking up in the mornings to Grandma passionately praying out loud as she walked around the living room, arms flailing, voice rising and falling as she switched between whispering and shouting the name of Jesus during her prayers. I remember piling into the car with all of my cousins every weekday during the summer and Grandma driving us to church camp. Oh, church camp. We followed the same ritual on Sunday mornings. Car. Us. Piled in. Church.

If Tiffanie, Mommie and Gram modeled for me what it was to be a Black woman saving other Black women—to the concept of a savior—then Grandma introduced me to Jesus as God. As divine. A God of liberation, the God who saves, and ultimately a friend. Not a grandpa in the sky who doesn't show up at all. You see, church wasn't the only place Grandma took us to experience Jesus. At least once per week my cousins and I would stand around the dining room table (barely able to see over it), waiting patiently as Grandma prayed and served us the body and blood of Jesus in the form of a wafer and grape juice. Grandma was serious about communion. Kind of in the same way Gram was serious about baptism. Grandma didn't just

13

use any old bread for our family communion rituals though. No way! She had the fancy church wafers. You know the nasty thin ones with the cross on them? That's what she would give us. We did however use Welch's Grape Juice to signify the blood. Standard. I remember Grandma repeatedly telling us the importance of taking communion often. I remember taking and feeling one with Grandma's God, and one with my sisters and cousins around the table. I remember feeling held and protected by something bigger than me, than us. Something divine. Something even bigger than Grandma! It just felt right.

Then magic happened. I was with Grandma and my cousins at an evening service at Grandma's church. The church was called Calvary Temple and Grandma was a well-known and active member there. I remember sitting to the left side of the center pew about midway to the back of the large church. I don't remember what the choir was singing or what the preacher was preaching but I do remember something pulling me to the front of the church. Was this Grandma's God? I got up from the pew and walked toward the altar. I stood there, eyes closed, surrounded by people but feeling like I was the only one in the room. And slowly, sweetly I began to feel an immense presence of love. I began to weep. I didn't move or even open my eyes because this love felt so good I didn't want to do anything to make the feeling go away. Moment after moment, waves and waves of this love washed over me. I didn't hear an audible voice, but deep inside me, I felt God saying, very sweetly, very motherly, "I love you." This love made me feel clean. It made me feel seen and wanted and beautiful and creative. It made me want to sing and dance and offer poetry. I remember saying to myself in that moment as tears fell from my cheeks to the ground, "This moment is how I will always be sure that God is real." In addition to my model for a savior, I now also had an imprint of a God.

I have never doubted God or Love since that moment. I started calling myself a Christian and I did what I thought Christians do. I read my Bible, prayed every night and even started trying to get my friends saved. I remember a couple of days later playing outside at my Auntie Cynthia's house with a friend. Playing quickly turned into me sitting her down on the curbside and telling her about Heaven and Hell. I told her that she needed to get saved so that she could spend eternity with Jesus in Heaven instead of burning for eternity in Hell. I scared her enough that she closed her eyes, held my hand and followed as I led her in what Christians call "the sinners prayer." I won't bore you with the details, but basically it's your ticket out of burning in Hell for eternity, and into a place in the sky with golden streets where everyone has their own mansion.

Oh yeah, and apparently Jesus is there too.

RAGE

Grandma was a hardcore Christian. But she wasn't exactly what I would call a "nice Christian lady." She could nag and yell, pretty much constantly. She and Grandpa were always arguing. I never remember a tender moment between them. It wasn't until she died that I realized how much they actually loved each other. Before then I always wondered why they didn't just get a divorce. But when it came to yelling, Grandma and Grandpa weren't the only ones wreaking havoc. The first time I heard the word "rage" we were doing laundry with Grandma at her house. One of my cousins did something that I thought was totally unfair. I don't even remember which cousin or what they did. But I remember being livid. I hated when things were not fair. So I went into an angry tirade with tears and yelling and all. I remember Grandma looking back at me from the washing machine and snapping, "You know, you have so much rage!" That word "rage" pierced me. I did not know what it meant, but I was pissed that I was being told that I had it. By this time my anger had grown to a point where it would completely take over me. I would go into a rage about the smallest things.

Once at my Dad's house in Georgia I was having one of my rage-full yelling fits. I was seething. Anger was pulsing through my veins. Again, I have no recollection of what had happened, but I know that I didn't think it was fair. I lashed out at my dad about it, then stormed down the stairs. I remember my stepmother saying as I passed by her, "I don't know how your dad lets you talk to him like that." Whatever I said, and how I said it, was a huge no-no for a Black mother. For most Black girls growing up, any expression of anger or rebellion was. And oh was I angry, and oh did I rebel. Rage, of course, was just absolutely unacceptable for a little Black girl. No matter what we have been through, that is not an emotion we are allowed to have. But every time it would rise in me, I just couldn't push it back down. My rage was a beast.

AS AN ADULT I realize the source of my rage: abandonment, neglect, sexual abuse, waiting for a mother who never came, my perpetrator being chosen over me, the lies and deceit. Shit, I had every right to be angry. And what made it worse is that I wasn't allowed to talk about Judy or Bill in my mom's house growing up. I wasn't allowed to ask questions even about the court case. Yes, there was a court case. Charges were pressed against Bill for what he did to me. I don't know what happened with the case even up until this day. My abuse and my time with Judy and Bill was like an elephant in the room that I felt too afraid to acknowledge. So I befriended the elephant. It became my darkness. A weight I carried with me always. But by looking around me, I saw that all of the strong Black women in my life—Mommie, Mom, Grandma, Auntie, my stepmother— were carrying the weight of their own elephants. So I came to accept that this was just mine to bear. But I didn't bear it with grace. And I didn't bear it quietly. I bore it the way I bore losing my first mother: arms flailing, tears streaming, screaming at the top of my lungs.

CHAPTER 3

Southern Girl

THE MOVE

When I was about ten years old Mommie moved us from our home town of Chicago to Marietta, Georgia. I was crushed when she told us we were moving. Chicago felt safe and familiar. Mom's was there, which had grown to be my anchor and safe place. The memories that lived there and the familiarity of the house wrapped around me like a warm blanket. I was already living life after Judy and life after Gram. I couldn't imagine a life so far away with Mom and Auntie. I didn't want to move. I didn't want our small family to break up. But Mommie had made up her mind, and before I knew it, we had moved down to Georgia.

The first few years in Georgia were hard but beautiful. The beauty emerged from the life my parents began to create for us. You see, my dad lived in Georgia, so although he was always a big part of my life, this move brought him and his family even closer. I also started creating beautiful friendships. Friendships that would become lifelong best friendships. More sisterhood. It's like the sisterhood of Black girls was following me everywhere I went.

The big problem was money. I have one memory in particular of driving around in our car, Mommie in the driver's seat, Tiff and I in the back, our clothes and small possessions stuffed in every crack of space we could find, riding around not knowing where we would sleep that night. I know this happened more than once, but I can't remember. Again, I think that may be on purpose. A vivid part of that memory is Mommie crying. I felt so sad for her, and I also felt guilty. During my childhood I felt guilty for being born. I felt like I was a mistake and a huge financial burden. I felt responsible for the financial issues we had. I even secretly felt that Mommie was angry at me for being born and thought that was the cause of some tension in our relationship.

In those days we would pay for gas in coins, usually putting in about two dollars at a time. We spent plenty of nights in dingy pay-per-night motel rooms that Mommie could just barely afford because we didn't have anywhere else to go but she was determined to give us a place to lay our heads. Then we graduated to living with other people who were kind enough to let us stay. We bounced around from one relative or friend's house to the next. Usually we were many people crammed into a small apartment. And then finally, we graduated to Mommie getting us our own places, but money was still always an issue. There was never enough. One utility or another was constantly being cut off. We got used to having running water but no electricity, or vice versa. Tiffanie and I became champs at doing our homework by candlelight and washing our clothes by hand with a gallon of water we got from the local Kroger for less than a dollar. We were evicted from more apartments than I can count. Our things thrown out onto the street like trash. And Tiffanie and I, filled with shame, standing watch over it so no one would steal anything. People would walk or drive by and stare as Tiffanie and I stood there guarding our things. Even friends from school would see and we felt so embarrassed. We would stand guard for as long as it took for Mommie to get her hands on enough money to rent a U-Haul truck to pack our things into. They cost nineteen dollars per day at that time. I still remember. We rented a lot of U-Hauls. We moved A LOT.

At that time I had no understanding of all the fucked-up systems that got us to where we were. I just saw Mommie, slaving away sometimes day and night, working so hard to keep a roof over our heads, but no matter how hard she worked or tried she just never could catch up on the bills. We just never had enough. I know it hurt her. She would cry every time another place was taken from us. I can only imagine what it must have been like for her: a single Black woman, without a college degree, two kids, in a brand new state where you have yet to build a support system. I don't know how she did it, but I am grateful that she did. I saw my mother try her hardest to give us a consistent place and fail to do so every time. I'm sure to her it must have felt like defeat. That's how I saw it then too. But as an adult I realize that it taught me a valuable lesson that has shaped my life: never give up. You are a Richardson woman. We never allow failure to have the final say.

No time for self-pity, no time to give up hope. You pick up your shit and you try again. Always.

When I was around twelve years old I remember being in the living room of our apartment with Mommie and Tiffanie. We didn't have any sofas or anything because we couldn't afford any, so we had made pallets on the floor to lie on and watch TV. I have fond memories of lying on the floor and watching Saturday morning cartoons. This day, Mommie got our attention and told us she had something to tell us. She was pregnant with a little girl! We were in complete shock but also beside ourselves with joy! All I could think of was how much fun I was going to have doing my new sister's hair. I could not wait to be a big sister! It wasn't until later that I realized how much more of a financial responsibility another child would mean for our family, and the magnitude of Mommie's choice to keep this baby.

I never remember my mother ever buying herself a new item of clothing or really doing anything for herself that cost money. When she had money, she always spent it all on us. But when she got to the point in her pregnancy that she could not fit into her normal clothes, I remember her buying one item of clothing for herself: a big pair of denim overalls. According to my memory, she wore them most of her pregnancy.

One day, I remember asking Mommie if we were still Christians because we didn't go to church anymore in Georgia. I remember her telling me "Yes, you don't have to go to church to be a Christian." I guess what I was really trying to ask is "Where the fuck is God in all of this suffering and lack? If God is real, why the fuck don't we have a home or money or running water? Why the fuck can't you afford to buy yourself another maternity outfit besides those goddamned overalls?" But instead, I just asked if we were Christians. I think this is the time in my life where I really began to pull away from God. I didn't get it. Life was hard. I was sad and angry. Mommie was crying all the time. And God was where?

I missed it. I had missed it again. I missed the miracle and glory in Mommie waking up every day and choosing us again and again. I forgot that this was the mystery of love and salvation. That no matter what, I choose you.

BEST FRIENDS AND HOOK UPS

When we arrived in Georgia I was in fifth grade and was enrolled at Brumby Elementary School in Marietta. Fifth grade was hugely impactful for me for several reasons. Not only was it my first time attending school in a new state, but I met three people who, unbeknownst to me, would change my life forever. The first are my two best friends, Natasha and Danielle. These phenomenal Black women are now my ride-or-dies. We've been best friends for well over twenty years. They've been teaching me about sisterhood and salvation the whole time. I'll never forget the way our friendship started. We were ten years old in our fifth grade classroom and Natasha called me a bitch. I was stunned. No one had ever called me a bitch before. I don't think I had ever even used that word before. Tasha was a spitfire from the beginning. Words like "bitch" flew off of her tongue easily. But that fire also makes her a passionate friend. She will literally do anything for her friends, for me. To this day, she has the dirtiest mouth and self identifies as "ratchet as fuck" which is great because she adds balance to my life. I need that ratchetness often and in large quantities. I need her in my life. Danielle has always been the more quiet one. She's also super smart. When we were younger she was kind of a pushover. She would let us convince her to stay out later than she wanted, to drink more than she wanted and to lie about it for us all. She's much different now. She's a professor at Spelman College with multiple degrees and she has sunk into herself in the most confident and beautiful of ways. She is an elegant, educated, deeply kind woman with a big heart for God. On a normal day when Tasha and I are downing margaritas one after another midday, she will ask for water and have no shame about it whatsoever. We also now know not to try to push her to drink more than she wants, or to do anything that she doesn't want to do. She has mastered the art of saying no. Tasha and I, on the other hand, draw a line when it comes to cocktails. We never say no to cocktails. Ever. Especially margaritas. So the three of us make a quirky but solid trio. Don't get me wrong though: Danielle will still out twerk us all if some old school dirty south music comes on.

The third person I met in fifth grade who would impact me forever was Ms. White. I loved her! I was very much a teacher's pet. She would allow me to sit beside her at her desk instead of in the main classroom area with the rest of the students. I just loved it. I remember always looking at her in amazement, especially her face. Her skin was smooth, and her lips were lush and I would stare at them whenever she laughed. She always wore her sandy brown hair down to cover what she called her big ears. Her voice and sweet southern accent were mesmerizing. I always had the desire to reach out to touch her, to stroke her skin. Little did I know, Ms. White was my fist innocent little crush.

Very soon after fifth grade came the "boy crazy" stage. I missed it, but my friends certainly did not. When we moved from elementary school to middle school we brought all our new curves and raging hormones with us. It began with kissing and touching in middle school and by the time we were in high school we were hooking up with boys and dating and talking about which boys we liked. By then we had also welcomed another friend into our crew. Her name is Laura, but we still affectionately call her by her childhood name: Laurita. We were no longer a threesome, now we were an unstoppable four! Natasha, Danielle and Laurita were always down to find ways to hook up with our teenage counterparts every weekend. Which we did. Unashamedly. We would all meet up at Danielle's apartment on Fridays after school. We would turn MTV on in the background (usually episodes of *The Real World* or music videos), talk pretty much all at once in a loud teenage gossip fest which only we could understand, apply make-up in the mirror, change and exchange outfits until we all felt our cutest, and the weekend would begin. We usually started at the local movie theater back when seeing a movie was cheap. But we weren't there for the movies. We were there for the boys. We would meet up with the boys there and usually go to the nearby Waffle House (a hole in the wall diner chain in the South) or to the bowling alley across the street. I don't remember ever bowling though. But the stairs in the back of the bowling alley was home to many of the fearsome four's hookups. One of us had our first experience being fingered on those stairs. Back then "getting fingered" was like a huge deal. Every time one of us would hook up with a boy, the first question we would all ask her before she could even get the story out was, "Did he finger you?" This was a big deal to us because it was the furthest we ever went when "hooking up" at that time. Back then we called anything before fourth base "hooking up." For those of you not familiar with the bases, in its heteronormative model fourth base was penis inside of vagina sex. We pushed the line but never crossed it. There were hookups in bathrooms, in the backseats of vans, in vacationing parents' bedrooms, on the stairs behind the bowling alley, in the movie theater, and the list goes on. After fingering the next big deal became oral sex. But of course it was all focused on male pleasure. The question we bombarded our sister/friend with when she came out of whatever hiding place where she was hooking up with a boy was, "Did you give him head?" And she would answer us with details you only share with people who are as close to you as we were to one another. She would tell us exactly how she did it, how he reacted, and even where she spit the cum after. I remember one time the answer being a plastic cup after one of us hooked up with a guy in the back of a soccer mom van. We were exploring our sexuality, our desire and our pleasure; and we had so much fun doing it. But I always felt like I couldn't quite get with the program. I always hoped my friends wouldn't notice, but rarely was I involved in hooking up with boys. I remember having crushes. One time I thought this boy was cool, so I wanted him to like me. I wanted his attention badly, to be validated by him, for us to be seen together and for me to be able to tell my friends that we hooked up. But I don't remember actually feeling that tingling sensation you get when you're attracted to someone when I thought of him or was around him. I pretended to be as excited about hooking up and meeting up with boys as my friends were, but I just wasn't. I liked the thrill and the excitement and the component of sneaking around behind our parents' backs, but there was always something a bit weird about my interactions with boys. It was like, I wanted to be seen like my friends were seen by boys. I wanted the attention, to feel wanted and beautiful. But that's pretty much all I wanted. Anything else I did was to keep the boys thinking I was desirable and to fit in with my friends.

But there did come a point where I couldn't hide behind my friends anymore. One day Natasha, Danielle and I decided to go over to a guy's house who lived in Danielle's apartment complex and stir up some trouble. Laurita wasn't there. This guy's mom wasn't home, and he had a group of guy friends over. This was the perfect situation for us to have some fun. We got there and decided to play Spin the Bottle. I don't remember much about the game, but I do remember it being my turn and the bottle landing on a boy named Corey. I was so nervous. I had never kissed anyone before. He was my first kiss. I can't really remember the kiss, but I remember the sense of pride I had at having done it. It felt so good to gab to my girlfriends about it as we walked home. We were all going on and on about what our kisses were like all the way back to Danielle's apartment. I remember the excitement being so high that we decided to invite the boys over again that night for the sole purpose of kissing again. The boy I had a crush on was amongst the boys who were invited over. The only problem was, we were not allowed to have boys over, and we certainly weren't allowed to just have a random make out session with them in the house. So, we made a plan. When we were at Danielle's house on the weekends we had a routine of locking ourselves in her room when we came home from our adventures and eating pizza and watching MTV. Usually the pizza was cold and from Friday night. We never bothered to warm it up. We even told ourselves it was better cold. So it was totally normal for us to be locked up in Danielle's room all night with sounds from the TV blaring. That night though, we decided to turn the TV up a little more than normal so Danielle's mom couldn't hear what was going on. We had told the boys to sneak in through Danielle's bedroom window and we would all kiss again. So when it was dark enough we opened the ground floor window of Danielle's bedroom and let them in. There was lots of kissing and then switching kissing partners and then more kissing. I remember kissing one boy that night: my crush. To my dismay, it was terrible! I felt like his tongue was assaulting me! When they left, climbing back out the window, I remember gossiping to my friends that he had "hurricane tongue." I felt disgusted. So kissing two boys in one day was pretty much the extent of my hooking up with boys, until one of my close friends told me he had a crush on me. Oh and by the way, about the window story, Danielle's older brother and his friends walked by as the boys were sneaking back out of the window and saw them. Yes, he told Danielle's mom. Yes, we were caught. Yes, Danielle got into lots of trouble. Her mom was furious and yelled at her in the living room. Meanwhile we were all just praying that she wouldn't call and tell our moms. She did not. So yes, in the end, it was worth it for all of us.

As I was saying, the next intimate interaction I would have with a boy was when I was a junior in high school and one of my close friends told me he liked me and wanted to date me. I was at his house for the purpose of telling him that my close friend liked him. He replied with, "But what if I like *you*?" It was smooth. It caught me by surprise. I never felt like I was attractive. I always felt that my friends and sisters were much prettier than me. They also wore makeup and knew how to dress well. I didn't do either of those things. So when this guy said this to me I felt really special and could not wait to tell Natasha, Danielle and Laurita. After his smooth line, he asked me if I wanted to be his girlfriend. My heart jumped! Someone actually wants to date *me*? This had never happened before! I said yes.

Seconds later I learned that basically us "dating" meant we had license to hook up. So he leaned in for a kiss and then there were tongues and bodies and sweat and breath everywhere. I didn't know what I was doing so I really hoped he liked it when we finished. As was our foursome's way, my friend and I did pretty much everything except "it." His penis never went into my vagina, but there was lots of pumping and grinding and touching and grabbing. I adjusted my clothes and prepared to leave after. That's when he dropped the bomb. He wanted to date me, but he wanted me to keep it a secret. He wanted to keep me a secret. I used to pretend not to know why, but I'm now old enough to admit to knowing that this boy just wanted to keep his options open, especially because so many girls liked him. And he was probably just horny that day and knew asking me to be his girlfriend would lead to a hook-up session. He and I dated for a total of about three weeks before he broke up with me.

I discovered during this "relationship" that I was terrible at hooking up with boys. I even tried oral sex quite unsuccessfully. His most frequent response when I tried was "ouch!" I never tried again after him. I would be in my thirties before I even began talking to my friends about oral sex with men again. We would sit around having drinks and they would explain the process to me. I would listen, very intrigued. We would laugh and use hand gestures. The closest I have ever gotten to trying again is in a dream I had in my thirties.

Natasha, Danielle, Laurita and I all went to separate high schools, but at first we spent every weekend together. Natasha and Danielle went to the schools they were supposed to go to according to their districts. Laurita went to a posh private school. That's when she began to drift away from us. I went to a magnet school for performing arts. As the years went by we began to make friends at our own schools and our weekends as a foursome became less and less frequent, but we had already built such a solid foundation that our love for one another was never affected. As we got older and would meet up sporadically at Danielle's on a Friday night to spend the weekend together, we stopped going to the movie theater or the bowling alley. We had begun partying by then, so we were always chasing the next party. We drank and some of us smoked weed. After a fun night we would sneak home and go straight to the bedroom to eat cold pizza and debrief the evening. Except for the time Laurita got so drunk she spent most of the night puking in the bathroom. Have you ever tried to puke quietly? It's a skill. We would grab slices of pizza and shove them into our mouth while asking each other all the important questions: *Who hooked up with who? Did you give him head? Was it good? Did he finger you?* But by then, I had figured out why hooking up with boys was never really my jam. At my high school I was having experiences that made things crystal clear.

CHAPTER 4

Queer Girl

HIGH SCHOOL DAZE

I went to a school called Pebblebrook High School. The magnet program that I was a part of was called CCCEPA (Cobb County Center of Excellence in Performing Arts). I felt in my element there, except for being one of the few Black students in the performing arts program. The students who went to the school because they were zoned for it were almost 100 percent Black, while the performing arts magnet students were almost 100 percent white. I remember the lunchroom literally being segregated. The district kids (Black) on one side, and the performing arts kids (white) on the other. I sat with the performing arts kids which was a bit awkward and uncomfortable. I would walk into the space and see a sea of black and a sea of white, and I would turn to the sea of white. Every time I made that turn it felt like a betrayal or denial of some sort. But at the time, all of my friends were performing arts students, so of course I wanted to sit with my friends. I guess I identified more deeply with my identity as an artist than with my identity as a Black person at the time. Identity was something I was reexploring during my days at Pebblebrook.

At first, I was a voice major. I loved learning arias and performing them for the class and hearing my fellow classmates do the same. I absolutely loved being a part of the chorus. I couldn't wait for our daily rehearsals. I would sing my heart out as I sat in the mezzo soprano section with my friends. We sang long scores of complicated music. I loved learning to sight read music and how to use my voice to make certain sounds for certain types of music or to hit certain notes. I loved learning what the pieces were about and wondering about the composers who wrote them. Of course my favorite piece to sing was Robert Ray's *Gospel Mass*. I especially loved the Credo movement of the mass. I remember holding back tears as my heart and throat burned while I sang with everything in me, eyes focused on the conductor, head bobbing to the rhythm, "I believe in the Holy Spirit and the Holy Catholic Church. I believe in the resurrection for the remission of sin and rebirth." And then finally at the end, belting out with the rest of the large chorus, "I believe in God! And in the Holy Ghost! I believe, I believe in God!"

"I believe." Such a powerful statement. As I sang it, it was as if my mind, heart and soul were in a civil war. I wanted to believe in Grandma's God but at that point in my young high school life, I was going through so much, questioning so much that I needed, I *needed* to proclaim that I believed anyhow. I needed to believe, and I needed to believe in God. So I sang it, and I sang it and I sang it, until it became more and more true. Even as I write this, I hear my heart shouting over the doubts in my mind: "I believe, I believe in God!"

One semester I decided to take drama as an elective course. My teacher's name was Mr. Adams. Within weeks of being a drama minor and vocal major, I knew I needed to switch. Mr. Adams soon pointed out that I was a natural on the stage and belonged in drama class. But I already knew. From the first class where we were introduced to what a monologue was and asked to memorize and practice one to be recorded as our "before" video (we would then watch them at the end of the year and see our growth) I loved it too much. Oh my God, I loved the idea of diving deep into a character and taking her on as myself. I loved that shit. I still do. I loved reading the words silently and hearing them in my character's voice, and then using my voice to make those words heard the way I heard them in my head. I loved feeling my character's emotions and using my body, voice and acting choices to communicate them to the audience. I loved playing with the text and finding little secrets in it. I loved breaking it down, marking all over the text with notes on where to take a beat or what my objective was and what tactics I was going to use to achieve it. Oh God, I loved allowing my character to take over my whole body. It was exciting to say things I wouldn't normally say, and to do things I wouldn't normally do. I reveled in making the character and her experience as real and true as possible. When acting, I let myself be completely free. It stimulated all of my senses.

I became obsessed with plays. I started reading them and soon I was getting cast in them.

In a play called *Durang/Durang* I was cast alongside a senior who we will call Kim. She was beautiful: dark skin, short hair, long brown fingers. She was a player. She was sleeping with all of my friends simultaneously and it wasn't long before I had my experience with her too. It was in high school, at Pebblebrook, that I started meeting people my age who identified as gay. This was exciting for me, but I wasn't exactly sure why at first. During this time I was becoming conscious that I might be gay, but it was something that was slowly creeping into my consciousness. The words "I think I'm gay" would creep up from my core into my brain as thoughts during times when I was by myself. Something weird would also happen whenever I saw same-sex couples or when I learned that an adult around me was gay. I would feel excitement and then a horrible dread that would cause me to cry. But even though I was having these experiences, when I got to Pebblebrook I didn't identify as anything outside of the heteronormative expectation society has for a high school freshman. But soon after arriving on campus, I began meeting the gays. I quickly learned which girls were lesbians. In addition to Kim, I was drawn to one senior with long red hair and a large nose. I was just drawn to them and curious about them. I would always try to get close to them and when I did, I would get awkwardly excited. This excitement felt good, and I wouldn't cry afterward anymore. I liked it. I wanted more of it. As time went on I began to feel that excitement around other girls too and even developed what I now know was a crush on my closest friend at school, Sadie. I didn't have a label for what was happening to me. I didn't even really know what this meant. But soon I was having daydreams of touching girls, seeing them naked, kissing them, our bodies touching. When I got close to girls like Kim I felt aroused; I longed for the fantasies in my daydreams to come true. I didn't share this with anyone and didn't think anyone noticed until one day on the school bus going home my friend blurted out to everyone around us on the school bus, "Brittanie is gay." I don't remember the context for this statement or how it came up at all. What I do remember is that everyone including both the long red haired hot girl and Kim heard. I felt an equal rush of embarrassment and a deep, deep "aha" moment. The thought of denying what my friend had said didn't even cross my mind. It actually felt like she had kicked down a door I had been trying to push open since I was ten years old. I remember smiling and confirming that, yes, I liked girls. Yes, "Brittanie is gay."

Oh, the freedom that came after this declaration! *That excitement I feel around attractive girls is called a crush. What my friends have been feeling for boys all this time, I feel about girls!* That's also when I realized with lots of cheekiness that Ms. White was actually my first crush. I felt liberated. I began letting myself feel what I felt.

My first sexual experience with a girl was with Kim. Again, I was kept a secret by her because she was also sleeping with all of my close friends. She told me not to tell anyone because she was trying to protect herself from being caught. I didn't tell anyone because I was pulling an asshole move sleeping with the person my close friend—well, friends—were madly in love with. I had a reputation of being a good girl, a great friend. So we kept it a secret.

Sex with Kim happened only once. But that's really all it took. It happened at her house in her bed, and it was nothing like I imagined. Kim lived with her mother and her grandmother who we laughingly called, "Grandma Weedy" because she grew weed in her closet. Kim got her hands on some of that weed one day and invited me outside behind her house. She lit the joint. I was nervous. I was sixteen years old but had never gotten high before or even been around someone getting high. This was before the fearsome four had been introduced to the land of weed. We were still in the land of learning to enjoy the taste of beers at parties. Kim took a few puffs from the joint and smiled, then she gave it to me. I was feeling all kinds of feelings at this point. I was a teenage girl super excited that the super-hot senior girl had invited me over for a sleepover. I was feeling very aroused and it only got worse as I watched her lips as she placed them around the small joint and then poked them out a bit as she exhaled. As I sat there, I kept my hands between my legs and tried to remember to breathe. When she handed me the joint I was hesitant, but I wanted to impress her, so I took a puff. Of course I coughed and she shushed me as we were smoking in secret. She also let out the cutest quiet laugh at me for not knowing how to smoke the joint. She showed me how to do it correctly, and then we went inside—to her bedroom.

Kim had the most beautiful singing voice. She sounded like Lauryn Hill. It was so smooth and rich and beautifully Black. When we got to her room she sat behind her keyboard and started singing. I was mesmerized and also quite high. I did not expect what happened next. At some point she stopped playing the keyboard, and turned on her stereo which played a cassette that was full of slow sexy jams. She turned the volume up high, turned around and looked at me hungrily, and the next thing I knew she was undressing me and kissing me. it was like my greatest fantasy had come true.

Now I would like to say it stayed like that. But it didn't. As we got into actually having sex I guess she forgot that she was super experienced while I had no experience at all with a woman. What she didn't know was that I also had a history of sexual trauma. The sex was painful. I mean, it hurt. I felt confused and unsure about what to do with my body. Everything she did to me was a surprise because I had never done this before so at each turn I would get scared of what she was going to do next. I had never thought about my relationship to sex because I had never had it. But here I was, having sex for the first time with a beautiful woman and all I could think of was things like, "What do I do with my legs?" and "Ouch, ouch, ouch!" I didn't say ouch out loud though because I did not feel I had permission to express my pain or even my pleasure. I had no context for having consensual sex (which of course is the only kind of sex, as non-consensual sex is rape). I had no context for prioritizing or even inviting my pleasure or my voice into sex. I was repeating what I had been taught through my abuse: to be preoccupied with her experience. To be completely obsessed with making sure she was having a great time. I did everything I knew, even if it hurt, to try to make her happy as our bodies engaged with each other's. I'm sure Kim had no idea this was happening inside of me. I am a great actress and I acted like everything was fine. Just like I had been taught to do as a child.

When we were done she pulled me up to her chest and wrapped her arms around me. I lay there feeling shocked and also a weird tenderness toward her. I guess vulnerability would be the right word. I had just had sex for the first time. At sixteen. With a woman. And now she is holding me against her breast. I tilted my head and looked her in the eye, she looked back at me tenderly, giggled and asked, "You want some more, don't you?" I couldn't work out what I wanted. I did not want more of the pain, but I did want more of something. I wanted more of her. We went at it again. This time was less painful, and I felt less awkward. I was less afraid as I knew what was coming. I relaxed into it a bit more. That's when the questions started. Can God still love me if I'm gay? Am I still worth saving and being kept safe if I like women? Would the Black women and girls that were showing up in my life keep showing up if I was different? Do saviors still save when you're gay?

ARTIST

My love for the arts didn't start at Pebblebrook. I discovered it as a little girl. I had an active imagination and drive for artistic expression. I learned how to use my imagination to escape my pain. I would create imaginary friends in my head who had all the attributes I needed. I used my imagination to create happy places. I would make up stories, I would even create little plays and force my cousins and sister to perform in them with me. My imagination soon morphed into great creativity. I began singing and writing my own songs. I often played conductor and forced my cousins to be in the choir. I would even make up dance routines and play choreographer while forcing my friends to be my dancers. Before I knew it I was also journaling a lot. Mostly about my fantasies and things that were in my imagination. It didn't take long for me to blossom into the identity of an artist; for "artist" to come first in my self-identification even before "Christian." I threw myself into art the same way I threw myself into Christianity at the altar at Grandma's church: completely. And similarly, just as my experience with God had, art completely changed my life.

When I was a young girl making up plays with my cousins, I didn't know how big a part of my life art would be. I started to think of art as a career path once I got to Pebblebrook. The chorus, *Durang/Durang*, and Mr. Adams's drama classes were not the only places I was having my insatiable hunger for artistic expression fed during my high school years. In fact, I would classify Pebblebrook as the secondary place. My main source of artistic fulfillment was coming from being a part of a theater company called the Freddie Hendricks Youth Ensemble of Atlanta (YEA). We were a group of youth led by artistic genius and creator of "The Hendricks Method", Mr. Freddie Hendricks. He led us in creating and performing original musicals based on social justice issues and ills around the world such as apartheid in South Africa, the HIV crisis that broke out in America in the '80s, teenage pregnancy, the epidemic of homophobia and more. Yes, Freddie molded us into great artists, but more important, he raised us to be great people. Like most YEA members, I look up to Freddie as my artistic father. He played a huge role in making me the person and artist that I am today. He demanded our best when we were acting, singing or dancing, but that didn't necessarily mean perfect technique for Freddie. He taught us that it means believing in our own inherent "greatness" and pushing ourselves past our insecurities and the things we believed we "can't" do. Freddie didn't believe in "can't." Freddie led us with love and into love. We learned to love ourselves, our craft, each other and the global community. Freddie challenged us to love instead of fear, to love instead of hate, to love instead of hide. When I joined YEA there were a lot of things I believed I "can't" do as an artist. Freddie pushed me to do all of them. In front of an audience. Repeatedly. It is one of the most loving things anyone has done for me. It built my self-confidence. Freddie also taught me about vulnerability. Vulnerability is the greatest lesson I have ever learned as an actor, so of course it came from one of the most vulnerable people I have ever met: Freddie Hendricks. I had built up so many walls to protect myself before joining YEA. I had packed all of my pain down deep inside and never planned on unpacking it, especially not with other people around. Freddie helped me lovingly let down those walls. I didn't need them anymore. I had built them to keep myself safe but Freddie had shown me how to use love to keep myself safe instead. To be open instead of closed even at the risk of pain. He taught me that it is okay to let the pain and the anger and the fear and all of that come out because love is more powerful and will always be there to catch you even in your own mess. And we were messes. Beautiful messes. We were a bunch of teenage messes with so much pain and trauma and need for love. But every Saturday we would come together at Lang Carson Community Center, and we would use our craft to open up, to let all our junk come out, to let love catch it all and transform it into something beautiful.

We created all of our own shows; from creating our own characters to creating the scenes. It all came from us. One unique thing about The Hendrick's Method is that we never used scripts. Freddie would always say "You wrote it, you know it!" So we created, rehearsed and performed full length musicals without a page of a script or even sheet music. The stories and songs were written from our hearts. That's where we got our lines and lyrics. Our dances were choreographed though. Our choreographer/dance teacher/uncle was named Charles Bullock. Charles was a tall, thin, handsome older man who loved to eat fried chicken at the director's table as he watched us during rehearsals. Charles took all of us, whether we were "dancers" or not and made us seasoned movers. I use the word "seasoned" intentionally as Charles is most famous for his feedback of, "That was good, but now put a little Lawry's on it!" American Black folk, I know y'all know what that means. But for the rest of you, Lawry's is a seasoning salt that Black people used to put on and in everything to make it taste good. Like Freddie, yes, Charles valued technique, but he valued our hearts more. He urged us to put our full selves into the dance moves, to push ourselves past comfortable, to *sweat*, to keep trying, to sink into our bodies and let them speak with the movement.

Every Saturday morning after warmups Charles would have us stand in three lines on one end of the rehearsal hall. The drummer would start playing a beat on the djembe. The energy of the room immediately shifted from the first strike of the drum. It was Charles's energy, it was our ancestors' energy, it was the energy of movement. As the drum sang we would begin our routine of dancing "across the floor." We would go three people at a time according to whoever was in front of the three lines. Charles would show us a dance move and then it would be our turn to do that dance from one end of the rehearsal hall to the other. Charles would watch us as we danced, full of energy, encouragement coming out of his eyes like a laser to each of us. When it was our turn we would dance across the floor using the movement that Charles had taught us, and if he didn't find what we did satisfactory, we would have to go back to the other end of the floor and do it again. Over and over, and over again. Until Charles was satisfied. Until he came and bowed before you and knocked on the floor praising you by saying "*a'jah boh*." I reached out to Charles to ask him what this meant. He told me that he learned the phrase while studying African dance. He connected to it and adopted it. He said,

"It means several things . . .

"*Ah* . . . " Yes. Indeed.

"Jah" Jehovah / God / Allah

"*Bo*" Bon. Good. Well done.

I loved Charles, but I hated dancing across the floor. In fact I hated dancing in general. I would become afraid and stiff when it was time to dance. Going across the floor is something I would begin to dread a week in advance. I was a person that frequently heard Charles yell "go back" over the drumbeat. So I would have to go back to the other end of Lang Carson and try again and again, usually tripping over my feet trying to get the footwork right, not sure what to do with my hands, and totally in my head thinking about how embarrassing this was instead of in my body trying to let the moves move through me. I was also usually crying. I have never been a good dancer. I think it has to do with being disconnected from my body for so long as a coping mechanism when Bill was sexually violating me. But in YEA there was no "can't." Everyone was a dancer. Everyone was an actor. Everyone was a singer. And if you weren't all those things when you came in, Freddie and Charles would pull it out of you, so you would be when you walked out.

Slowly but surely as the weeks went on, dancing across the floor became less about being embarrassed about how I looked and more about my relationship with myself and my body. With Charles's encouragement I began sinking into my body and got out of my head. I began to focus on the experience of my body in movement instead of focusing on the way it looked to others on the outside. After a while, dancing even started to feel a little good! I got to a point where sometimes, just sometimes, I would go across the floor once without hearing "go back" and even hearing "*a'jah boh*" when I found myself at the other end of the rehearsal hall. Don't get me wrong, I never did become a great dancer. Choreography is still hard for me. I still sometimes trip over my feet. But I trust my body. I feel good in my body. I enjoy moving my body and trying. I feel more connected and inside of myself. Sometimes in dance classes I still cry, but it's not because I am embarrassed to be the worst dancer (which I usually am), but because I am so deep inside of my body that tears of relief or pleasure fall. They are now healing tears. My body and I are still reconciling, and movement is one of the greatest healing tools I use to facilitate that process. I have Charles to thank for that.

At the end of every YEA workshop or rehearsal we did the most important thing. We stood in a big circle, held hands, bowed our heads and prayed. We offered gratitude to God for our gifts, for our love, and for our time together. We asked for what we needed. And then again ended in thanks. Once "amen" or "*ashe*" was said by all: the youngest member to the oldest member, the most talented to the least, we all bowed, and knocked on the floor. This was a sign of gratitude and reverence to ourselves, to one another, our ancestors, our creator, and all of creation.

CHRISTIAN OR LESBIAN?

By the time I was sixteen, my schedule had become too much for either of my parents to be able to drive me around every day. So my dad graciously bought me a little car to get me back and forth to all my rehearsals, school, and work. My first car was a greenish-bluish Ford Contour. My dad had bought it at an auction for $800. It was an old car, and I definitely beat it up with lots of dings and scratches, but she got me where I needed to go. I named her "Ms. Butch" as a friend and I decided that of course my car had to be a butch lesbian, especially with all she had to do. Monday through Friday I would go to school. After school we had chorus rehearsal. Then after rehearsal my friends and I who were also YEA members all piled into Ms. Butch and raced to YEA rehearsal which happened from 6:00 to 9:00 p.m. when we were preparing for a show. After rehearsal I would drop friends off to their respective locations and head home. Or sometimes the whole cast would all meet at Fellini's Pizza on Ponce de Leon Ave and stuff our faces while loudly making jokes and talking about things that happened in rehearsal that day. We also had YEA workshops and rehearsals on Saturdays. On Sunday we rested. I loved this. I loved the pace. I loved the community that was created. I loved being constantly involved in doing my art. My whole life was basically acting, singing and dancing; or thinking about acting, singing and dancing. During seasons where we didn't have evening rehearsals I had an afterschool job at a Mexican restaurant. I started off as a hostess and moved to being the to-go server. This is how I paid for gas for Ms. Butch as well as those slices of Fellini's pizza. As I worked, packing to-go orders or walking guests to their tables, I would often rehearse in my head. I would get to work, say hi to everyone, and then start singing the entire musical we were currently working on from start to finish under my breath. It made the time pass faster and it made working more fun. It became such a habit that years later, I still find myself singing the songs under my breath. As I've grown I've learned to see this as a miracle, as divine: the fact that I always kept on singing.

This time in my life was pretty blissful. Along with my besties (Natasha, Danielle and Laurita) and my YEA family I had also made some great friendships at school. So many precious friendships that I cannot name them all here. Not that you all care to read a list of all my friends from high school. But my friends became my chosen family. Especially since Mom and Auntie were now so far away. I needed a place to belong and found it in YEA and in my friendships. By the time I joined YEA I was out to all my friends from Pebblebrook. As soon as I entered the YEA space I immediately knew it was safe and a place where I could be my full self, so I came out through a piece I wrote and performed during a YEA workshop. Apart from the questions about God and salvation, I had become comfortable with my sexuality and even enjoying going through my late blooming girl-crazy stage. My biggest crush at the time was Janet Jackson. A poster of her half naked hung on my bedroom wall. At this time I had a couple close friends who also liked girls, who identified as bisexual. Kim had slept with most of them. One of them was also a YEA member, so we spent lots of time together. We were together at school, at YEA, and all the hours spent in Ms. Butch, traveling between the two. This friend who we will call Kristin and I became close. She was bisexual, so we would talk a lot about girls and our crushes and our secret escapades with girls. It was lots of fun. But then something changed. Kristin became very close with an older YEA member named Keith. Keith was a devout conservative Christian young man. Because Kristin had also come out to our YEA community, Keith knew that she liked girls.

Keith began to have intense talks with Kristin about her "sin," her "sexual immorality." He preached to her about how she needed to repent from homosexuality, to ask God to change her orientation, for her to resist her attraction to women and become straight for God. He taught her that if she really loved Jesus (which she did), she would "leave this gay lifestyle" and live as a straight woman as the Bible required. These talks became a thing. Kristin became involved in Keith's mission to pray the gay out of her and make her choose to be straight. She started going to church things with him and they would hang out and study the Bible verses that say homosexuality is a sin. Soon enough Kristin had been converted. There was no more talk about girls. Only Jesus. All. The. Time.

Now, since Kristin and I were so close, I of course also got pulled into the situation. I began to feel "convicted" as we say in Christianity, about my "sin" of being gay. To be more clear, being *happily* gay. The questions all came back. What Keith was teaching Kristin and the conviction she had to change started rubbing off on me, but I wasn't as easy a convert as Kristin. Along with these feelings of condemnation, I began to reason that God and I were good. We didn't have any beef, just love. But it was hard to stay convinced of that. Around this same time Mommie also had a come-to-Jesus experience. We started going to church on Sundays. Before I knew it, Christianity had become a big part of my life again. We were no longer Christians who didn't go to church. We were now Christians who went to church Sunday and Wednesday and who boasted about the goodness of Jesus and how blessed we were to be saved. This made me feel backed into a wall: I had to choose if I was a Christian or a lesbian.

At my mom's church one day, during the Wednesday evening youth service, I rededicated my life to Jesus as the pastor instructed. Let me set the scene for you. It was dark and the keyboard was playing softly, everyone's hands were raised in praise to Jesus and their eyes closed with tears of devotion falling down. The pastor spoke in the microphone with a smooth wooing voice: "The time is now to get saved." He said that we have the choice to spend eternity in Heaven or in Hell. In Heaven we would get to be with Jesus, the lover of our souls. There would be no more pain or sorrow in Heaven. We would be with God. Or we could choose not to get saved which means we would go to Hell. There we would burn in flames of fire for all eternity. We would suffer for all of eternity without relief. The only way to keep ourselves from going to Hell was if we "accepted Jesus into our hearts" right now. I was scared as hell. I thought about the feeling of burning in fire forever and I knew I definitely did not want that. I thought Jesus was already in my heart and I thought God was love, not fear. But I couldn't risk it. Hell sounded horrible. So I decided to make a choice. I raised my hand when he asked who was ready to get saved today, to choose to spend eternity with Jesus instead of in the fire of Hell. After several of us teens in the large dark room raised our hands, he led us in the "sinners prayer." We prayed for God to forgive us for our sins and for Jesus to come into our hearts and be our Lord and savior. We told God that from that point forward we would live for Him and turn from our sinful ways. Then we said amen. We opened our eyes, and everyone clapped for us and even screamed with joy. We had all just been saved from Hell by Jesus. Everyone was so happy for us. I didn't feel happy at all. I was scared shitless. I was anxious to hurry up and get out of that building so I could "turn from my wicked ways" and obey the Bible. I needed to tell all my friends too. They needed to come to church with me and get saved or they would burn in Hell for eternity. Before that night I hadn't really thought much about Hell. Especially not the burning forever part (that's the big whammy for me as you can probably tell). God was that loving presence I felt at the altar at my Grandma's church. That love and peace was what I had focused on really. But Hell changed everything. I was like "Fuck this God-loves-me shit. God is judging my every action and if I mess up I'm going to Hell so I need to get my act together." I started striving to be a "Good Christian" in the way that my mom's church and Keith and Kristin taught. I wanted to go to Heaven. Actually it wasn't even about going to Heaven, I didn't want to go to Hell.

By this point I had become good friends with a girl we'll call Dee. Throughout most of high school Dee was dating her longtime boyfriend. Over time Dee and I got really close. One Wednesday she invited me to her house so we could go to church together and then I could stay for a sleepover. I said yes and was super excited. Memories of the actual service fail me. But I do remember that I really loved being at Dee's house. It felt like being a part of a family. She had an older sister and younger brother. Her parents were happily married. Her mom was usually at home, so I have memories of sitting around the table with her and Dee talking, probably about Jesus. This wasn't the kind of savior I had seen in my mom, sister and friends. This was Jesus who saved you from Hell. I once again became convinced that they were different. Dee and I began going to church together often, but there is one night at church that I will never forget.

I was struggling with my sexuality. I was being taught that being gay was a sin and I didn't want to sin because I didn't want to go to Hell. But my feelings for girls were not going away. I would go back and forth between enjoying expressing my sexuality by wearing my rainbow beaded pride bracelet one day and then feeling like a sinner who needs to repent the next. I wanted to change for God out of fear of Hell, but out of love for myself I wanted to be who I knew I was. But the church was teaching us to love God above all, and that our fleshly desires were sinful and needed to be prayed away. So I chose to love God instead of myself. Well, at least I tried to.

One evening I joined Dee's family at a church. It seemed a bit farther away than their usual church. I guess it must have been some sort of special occasion or revival or something. When we arrived, Dee and I sat next to each other. I don't remember much of what happened in the service except for the end. Lights down, keyboard playing, people's arms raised worshiping Jesus and crying out of devotion to Him. I think you get the drift by now. This time though Dee and I were a part of the people with their hands raised in worship. We were saved. We were Christians. We loved Jesus and we were going to Heaven. Or were we? As the keyboard played the pastor got on the mic and invited people to come up for prayer. He said that if we were struggling with anything and needed prayer, needed Jesus to help us, we should come forward right now. My stomach dropped and I started to cry. The pastor continued, "Come, come right now. Jesus is available for you." I was in so much turmoil. I felt like I was being called by the Holy Spirit to go up and get prayed for, but I was afraid. I was maybe sixteen years old at the time. I was embarrassed to go up to the line of people standing in front of the altar, choose one, and admit to that person that I knew I was "a homosexual" and that even though I was trying not to be anymore, it wasn't working, and I needed Jesus to help me change. I needed to be saved from my gayness. With tears streaming down my face and guilt and shame weighing on me like a ton of bricks, I squeezed past everyone in my pew and walked up to the front. When I got to the altar, worship music in the background of my sobbing, I lifted my head and found myself in front of an older white woman. She leaned down to my ear and asked me kindly, "What do you need prayer for?" Then she turned her head and put her ear close to my mouth so she could hear me. My throat was tight. I felt like I had no air to breathe, but somehow I pushed out the word "homosexuality." She took my hands in hers and prayed a prayer that I don't remember. But when she finished, I walked back to the pew convinced that I was cured. That same night I destroyed my beaded rainbow bracelet, I was new now. I was cured. I was no longer a homosexual. Jesus was happy with me. I had been saved from homosexuality by Jesus. I was not going to Hell for sure this time.

CHAPTER 5

Lover Girl

WORKING

Before I knew it high school was ending, and it was time for me to go to college. What to major in wasn't even a question. I knew I wanted to study acting. Auditioning for school was a whirlwind. In our world, SAT scores and community service hours didn't really matter. It was all about talent. I worked extra hard on my audition pieces, not only because I wanted to get into a good school, but also because I knew that I couldn't actually afford these colleges that I was auditioning for. So I wouldn't just need to be good, I needed to be what Freddie taught me to be: "great" so that I could also get talent-based scholarships. My hard work, the work of all my teachers at Pebblebrook and YEA, and all the hard work and sacrifice of my family paid off! I was accepted to University of the Arts in Philadelphia, one of my top choices. Not only was I accepted but I was offered lots of financial aid as well as a huge talent-based scholarship. These two things combined covered most of the cost of my tuition at the coveted school. To cover the rest and pay my rent and living expenses I worked when I wasn't in class. I worked a lot. I served tables and bartended throughout college. My junior and senior year I also ran an afterschool program for youth in a homeless shelter called the Red Shield in Philadelphia. There was even a year where I was working three jobs in addition to going to school in order to support myself and pay my tuition payments (I was on a monthly payment plan).

Waiting tables and bartending was purely for making money. I actually made very good money in that industry. A plus was that I made lots of friends with whom I had lots of fun while doing it. Like most restaurant employees, once we closed down the restaurant we would all go out to our favorite bars in Center City Philadelphia, squeeze into booths or sit around big tables, and order pitchers of beer and shots. We'd laugh and drink until the bar closed. We of course always tipped stupidly well, as we were service workers ourselves. Then, depending on the night, we would either go home or we would go to the local hole in the wall after-hours bar to keep drinking and laughing and relieving the stress of our shifts. We talked shit about the shitty customers we had served that day or bragged about our highest tipping customers. We talked about who could cover who's shift when, for one reason or the other. We shared our opinions on the managers and the newly hired employees who weren't cool enough to be invited out with us after work just yet. Some people formed romantic relationships based on our after-hours socializing. Some of us became best friends. But mostly we were just there to create a space for ourselves to unwind after the hectic experience that is a shift (or double shift) as a service worker at busy Center City bars and restaurants.

I usually worked at the Red Shield after classes and before going to bartend. I started there as just a volunteer, but before I knew it I was directing the program. This is a pattern in my life. I used to feel guilty for it, but I am learning not to. I am a natural leader. It's just the way I was created.

The Red Shield was my first "big girl" job and the first job that I felt really ushered me into my destiny. I loved being there. I loved the people there, I loved the work that I did, I loved my boss, and most of all I loved the kids I worked with. They were my first "kids." Spoiler alert: lots more to come. The Red Shield was much more than a job for me. I was fully invested in those kids and went over and beyond to give them some slices of happiness in their lives while they were experiencing the trauma of homelessness. At a minimum, my job was just to educate and entertain the kids for a couple hours after school in an upstairs room at the shelter, take my paycheck, and go back to my privileged life. But getting to know these kids and hearing their stories—how their experiences had been limited to trauma and how they had access only to a small part of the world (most often just a small part of the city)—furthered my education. I saw that having fun and other childhood experiences to which they had every right just weren't prioritized in their lives. Pain, loss and constantly being kicked down to the bottom of the ladder took up too much space. There wasn't much time left in the day to just be a kid. I made it my personal mission to rectify this in whatever ways I could.

Often, we went to the park and had a pizza party or rode the subway (all the kids in tow) to museums, art galleries or events I had gotten free tickets to. I remember hosting a big dinner for them at an Italian restaurant where I worked. They got all dressed up and came for a fancy meal. None of them had ever been in such a nice restaurant before. They had a blast. They took up as much space as they wanted with no apologies! I advocated for them whenever I could. I tried to expose them to as many opportunities as possible. Holidays were always fun. I remember decorating the room and handing out candy for Valentine's Day and surprising them with a Christmas party at my school where they all were showered with love and gifts from the Black Student Union. Sometimes we stayed in and had fun. We would watch movies together or play outside in the gated area in the back of the shelter on days when the weather was nice. These afternoons, as I watched kids play ball or jump rope, I made the deepest connections with them. Inevitably one would come sit next to me just to talk. Just to share with me what they were going through. We made the most precious memories and loved one another deeply. My program wasn't only about field trips and playing outside, though. The kids also worked hard academically. I remember creating games to help them with their math and science. One of my students came into the program unable to read, and I remember spending countless hours with him, book open, sounding out words. I brought in help from my classmates at UARTS to tutor the kids with their homework. Usually, after homework they journaled. I introduced them to a journaling practice that helped them with their writing skills and also worked as a therapeutic tool. Then came the fun activity of the day.

I remember when I was gearing up to go to South Africa for the second time (I had gone once in high school), I took the kids on the journey of preparation with me. We pulled out maps and globes and learned about where I was going. We watched movies and read about South Africa. The kids were amazed at how big the world was. Most of them had never left their community. None of them, even the children of the mother who had fled the war in Liberia and landed homeless at the Red Shield, had ever been out of the country or even thought of traveling outside of the country as an option. We also worked through the mutual grief we were feeling about being separated from one another during my time away. These kids were my world, my whole heart. I was deeply satisfied by my work and believed in the importance of it.

Being in a relationship with families that are experiencing homelessness was not all roses, obviously. As I said, we created slices of happiness together, but to some extent, my program was not the reality these children faced. It was more of an escape from their realities. I was trying to expose them to what their future realities could be, but for now, they were kids without homes who were experiencing trauma and their reality was that food and shelter were not always guaranteed. So, plane tickets to South Africa or bus fare to go to an art gallery wasn't even on their radar. It was a life to hope for and work toward, but it was not their current reality. Sometimes I sit back and wonder how helpful, if at all, it was to take kids experiencing poverty to posh restaurants and provide them Christmas gifts their own parents could not afford. Thinking about that makes me anxious and fearful. It makes me worry that I was perpetuating the white savior complex or that I was just flaunting my privileged life in these kids' faces and then dropping them back at the homeless shelter where they lived. But when I think deeply and meditate on this, I always come back to the same place. A place of peace. I am at peace with the work I did at the Red Shield. Could I have done it differently and in a more conscious way? Definitely. But you can't give what you don't have. I wasn't as conscious back then. I was also very young. But being a person who has experienced both childhood trauma and homelessness, and the trauma that comes from homelessness (though my experience was very different as I never had to live in a homeless shelter), and just being a survivor of the darkness, I look back and appreciate the slices of hope that were offered to me, the slices of happiness, the people who came in and gave me a break from my pain, the people who showed me a world bigger that I ever had imagined. They groomed me into the wild dreamer that I am and taught me not to stop dreaming. They gave me the hope I needed to take the risks necessary to make my own dreams come true. People like Denise Vazquez Troutman who took me into her home for a while and in addition to radical love and acceptance, offered me a life of going to fancy restaurants and shopping for brand new clothes at Marshalls. Things I didn't do otherwise in my new life without Auntie and Mom. I am grateful for these experiences; they challenged me to believe that my life could be different. I remember Denise saying to me one time when she asked if we wanted to join her at the grocery store, "Brittanie, whenever you have the opportunity to go somewhere, even if it's just the grocery store, go!" This statement would carry me into adventures across the country and the globe. I find peace in the possibility that I was able to do the same for the children in my program at the Red Shield.

Peace isn't my biggest takeaway from my experience there though. The Red Shield was also where my blinders began falling off a bit. It's where I began realizing something that would become more and more apparent to me as I got older and saw more of the world: the system is fucked up. The Red Shield was a safe, respectful, equitable place from what I could see. It was a place with a zero-tolerance policy for violence. Trauma-informed care was practiced and each family had a caseworker (with a small caseload) who helped them make and achieve goals toward emotional stability and self-sufficiency. Three free meals a day were provided, and living in the shelter was free. But for its residents, this world was not their world. Their stay at the Red Shield was only temporary, and their lives didn't begin at intake.

During my time there my relationships with two families stick out most prominently. One was with a young mother who was almost my age. I was about twenty-two at the time. She had four children and lived in one of the Red Shield's rooms with her kids. The more I got to know her and her children (including the one who was almost always glued to my hip), the more I realized that in most ways she was like me, except for the fact that she wasn't born into the privilege I had been born into. I had grown up with the care of Black women who loved me, I had best friends I could always depend on for support, I was able to access education all the way through high school, get my diploma and then attend a college in a totally different state. I was so employable that I had three jobs! This also gave me economic privilege. At least once per week I would get off of work, go to the 7-11 by my house and buy whatever I wanted with the big stack of cash I had made from bartending that night. I bought snacks, usually the sweet and salty Chex Mix, a pint of birthday cake flavored ice cream, some sort of candy bar and whatever else tickled my fancy that day. I would also walk across the street to the liquor store and buy myself wine or beer, whichever I had a taste for that day. Then I would walk back across the street to my studio apartment on Chestnut Street in the heart of Center City Philadelphia, say hello to my doorman and step into the elevator that carried me up to my floor. I would go into my apartment, change into the most comfortable clothes available or none at all, sit in my huge bed that was just for me, and watch cable TV as I ate my snacks and texted back and forth on my cell phone that I had to replace frequently because I would often throw it across the room in anger as I knew I could always just buy another one. So no, this woman and I were not the same. Our experiences were totally different. My point is that she was smart and inherently had everything I had to be successful, but she hadn't been protected from the blows of capitalism, misogyny, classism, racism, sexism, systemic poverty and the destruction of self-worth and self-image like I had been. The difference between us was that the system had fucked her over more than it was able to fuck me over. I wasn't smarter than her or more hard working or less in love with booze than she was. I had just been protected. I had just been privileged. This realization would shape the rest of my life.

This may have been the first time that I realized that because Black women starting with my sister had reached back and saved me, I was able to reach forward and help liberate others. I began to realize that maybe I too was a sister savior. Maybe I too could help further liberation in the world. Maybe I could reach out and grab a Black woman's hand and say, "I got you." Our liberation was all wrapped up in each other's. As Emma Lazarus wrote, "Until we are all free, we are none of us free."

Maybe my life wasn't just about me being saved and kept safe, but also about me doing the same for others.

IN COMES ITTY

I remember arriving in Philadelphia to begin my four-year acting degree at University of the Arts. I was so excited! My dad and uncle flew up to Philly with me to get me all settled into my dorm. They took me shopping to buy all the things I needed for my dorm room. UARTS actually only had apartment style dorms. So we bought all the things I needed, and I moved in.

What made arrival day at UARTS even more exciting and less intimidating was that two other Pebblebrook graduates were also entering the university that year. They were both dance majors. One was one of my closest friends (and senior prom date) Justin, and the other was a girl named Katie. I didn't know her well but we would become great friends. After we were all moved in we said goodbye to our families and began our first night as free adults in college with our own apartments. We wasted no time breaking rules and fully enjoying our freedom. I stuck to Justin like glue that night. He took me to his dorm where I met his roommates. Then he invited me to come with him to Katie's room to see her and hang out. We got to Katie's room and squealed and hugged each other and then just sat around and talked excitedly about the new journey we were about to embark on. Katie's roommates were also there so we met them. They were all pretty nice (at least then they were) as Katie introduced us to them. But then she introduced us to her final roommate: a short, white girl with a gorgeous face, slightly baggy jeans, her dark hair hanging straight down underneath a Philly's fitted cap that was slightly cocked to the side. She had a nervousness about her that made her bounce a little when she walked and do this really cute little sniff thing where her nose twitched up to the side when she was in conversation and didn't know what to say or when she was meeting new people. But she also had this confidence about her. Unlike us, Philly was her home. She had grown up there. Her family's home was just a short drive away. So, this really wasn't that big of a deal to her. She smoked Newport cigarettes and rocked large hoodies over her tiny body when she would take smoke breaks. By now you have probably figured this out, but we had a problem here: Hannah was *hot!* She was the hottest girl I had ever seen. When I looked at her my body started doing all kinds of crazy things. *"No!"* I thought. *"No! I'm not gay anymore. I'm cured. This isn't happening!"* Hannah didn't have to come out to us. We all just assumed she was gay. I tried my best to hold my shit together. I was thinking *"I will not be coming back to this room."* I knew just by looking at Hannah that she was dangerous territory for me. I knew just by looking at her small face with those gorgeous green eyes, that I could fall deeply in love with her. I didn't want to. I wanted to be straight for Jesus. I tried to just pay close attention to Justin and Katie and look as straight as possible (which isn't hard for me). But then Katie blurted out "Oh Britt, so was the whole gay thing just a high school phase for you or are you still a lesbian?" I can't remember how I responded or what happened after that. But days later, those green eyes had become my home, the first place I had really felt at home since being snatched away from Judy's house. I didn't fall in love with Hannah. I leapt into love with her. I leapt with my arms and heart wide open, loving what I saw as I descended deeper and deeper. And I wasn't alone. Hannah was there with me leaping as deeply into me as I was into her. I know the sight was also beautiful for her because she told me so often. Until meeting Hannah, I never knew what it was like for someone to find you so beautiful that you took their breath away. For years, Hannah could not look me in the eyes for long because when she did she would literally forget to breathe. When she realized it, she would go through the same ritual every time: she would avert her eyes from mine quickly, grab her chest with her right hand

and bend down to catch her breath, left hand on left knee. And then she would say breathlessly "you are so fucking beautiful."

Being with Hannah was like a dream. When I told Justin that we were dating, he literally jumped up from his seat and said, "Oh my God Britt, you are dating the hottest girl in school!" I loved being Hannah's girlfriend. I don't really remember ever not being. Like most lesbians our age, we "u-hauled" immediately. I don't remember her asking me out on a date or vice versa. I do not remember us deciding to be a couple. I just remember being hers and her being mine—and being wildly happy about it. I do remember the first time we had sex. Well, I remember what happened after. We were in her dorm room on the futon she slept on in the living room. All the beds were in the bedroom but because she was an insomniac she slept outside the bedroom on this old black futon. We were lying there, and she sat up, opened the window and picked up her orange fish shaped bowl. Not the kind of bowl you eat out of, but a small glass bowl for smoking weed out of. Orange was her favorite color. And even though it was dark I remember smiling at how the moonlight shone on her thin lips as she puckered them into the shape of the glass fishy to wrap them around the bowl and take a hit. She inhaled the smoke and then blew it out of the window. Weed smoking obviously was not allowed in the dorms, but Hannah was a rule breaker. After she exhaled she turned to me, her neck a little straighter and her nervousness completely absent. She was like a solid rock. "*My rock,*" I thought. She turned to me after this first time of love making and said to me, "I'm going to marry you one day." Then she turned back to her bowl, lit it up again and inhaled, blowing the smoke out of the window. I didn't just feel butterflies in my stomach, I felt them in my heart, in my throat, in my toes. My whole being was buzzing. I felt so happy and excited. Not only was I dating the hottest girl in school, and not only was she the most amazing person I had ever met, but she was also going to marry me. Life felt like it couldn't get better.

I don't know if it was the next day or several weeks later, but one night Hannah and I were chilling on the futon. As usual, she was wide awake in the middle of the night. Her insomnia always kept her up all night. So naturally I also began staying up at night. Too excited to spend as many moments with her as possible to leave her and go to sleep. It was the middle of winter in Philly; outside it was freezing and snowing. One of my favorite things about Hannah was that she was very spontaneous. I would get to savor that spontaneity this night. She told me to get dressed: big winter coat, gloves, hat, the works because we were going somewhere special for an impromptu photoshoot. Hannah was studying photography at UARTS and back then was almost always taking pictures or hanging out in the darkroom developing them. This was before the digital camera age. So we got all bundled up and went on what I think was the most romantic date we ever went on in our entire relationship. It was free. It was just she and I. And it was perfect. She took me to a secret place of hers which I remember to be the top of a building that was just covered in snow. I hate winter. I hate snow, but with Hannah, I loved anything, even being cold. I was amazed at how beautiful the untouched snow looked. It was just a huge rooftop thick with clean white snow. And then, we played. We played in the snow. And Hannah took pictures of us doing it. We laughed. We drew hearts in the snow. We made snow angels. We wrote things like "Hannah loves Britt " in the snow. We kissed, our freezing lips finding warmth against each other's. We were up there for what seemed like forever, in Hannah's secret place, playing in the snow and enjoying being in love. Just the two of us. Grown women. Completely sober. Playing and loving, and taking pictures along the way. Hannah later developed those pictures and put them into a photo album. Our guards were completely let down that night. I would say that was probably the night Hannah became more than my lover, more than my best friend. She became "my person." I was all of me with her.

Very soon Hannah and I became known as "the lesbians." I think Katie lovingly adorned us with this nickname. We were no longer Hannah and Brittanie, two separate humans. We were "the lesbians." We would walk into bars (underage at the time) and friends would yell to us "Lesbians!" then turn to their group and say things like "look, the lesbians are here!" and we would go over and hug everyone and start drinking shitty beer together. I would usually be seated on Hannah's lap, but that wasn't enough PDA for us. We also had to be holding hands. We couldn't get enough of each other and didn't give one fuck what anyone thought. We were always holding hands or showing affection anywhere: walking down the street, in the pizza shop, at parties, wherever. Facebook had also come out by then, and our pages were full of pictures our friends had posted of us kissing and embracing at random places, not knowing people had a camera pointing at us. But we didn't care. We were in our own little love bubble and life was good there. At least it was for us. Soon I had basically moved into Hannah's small dorm room with her which means I was an extra body in a small room where four people were already squeezed in. So we would often hear

SISTER SAVIOR

her roommates shout at us, "Lesbians, stop laughing so loud. It's 3:00 a.m. and I'm trying to sleep." Or "Lesbiaaaaans! God, must you take a shower together? You literally spend every moment together. Get out! I need to shower and go to class." Or "Lesbians! I can literally hear you swapping saliva around the corner. It's gross. Stop!" That was pretty much our freshman year in college. Hearing "Lesbians!" screamed at us by our friends over and over followed by them telling us to stop doing something annoying that we were very guilty of doing.

Hannah was my first real relationship and I remember when I wanted to start calling her "baby" but I was too nervous. I had never called or been called such an endearing romantic term by anyone. But it was coming naturally to my lips and I wanted to let it out. So I came up with a solution, the corniest solution ever, but it stuck. As I keep reminding you, Hannah was tiny. Everyone was always commenting on how short and skinny she was. One night I casually said (as if I hadn't been rehearsing it in my head for days), "Hannah, you are so small. You are tiny. You are little. Like an itty bitty baby . . . . " Nervous laughter followed. "Can I call you "Itty Bitty Baby"? From that night on "Hannah" became only "Baby" or "Itty" to me. Those are the only two things I called her for years. I even bought her a silver heart shaped necklace with her new nickname "Itty" inside of the heart. She wore the necklace every day without ever taking it off.

In true young lesbian fashion, it wasn't long before we decided that I needed to meet her dad. So, one Saturday we invited him over for pancakes. We all ate pancakes and had a great afternoon together. That was the first time I met her dad, Louis. He would soon become a very special person in my life along with Itty's mother, Catherine. At the pancake brunch Itty never introduced me to her dad as her girlfriend. She waited until he left and then told him over the phone. His reaction was anticlimactic, in the best of ways. He said something like "She seems like a great girl, I'm really happy for you two." My gender was never a problem for Louis and Catherine. They didn't even blink an eye at it. Itty's previous long-term relationship was with a guy, this one was with a girl. Nothing about that seemed like anything to make any kind of fuss over. It was like she had told them the sky was blue.

Itty, Catherine and Louis didn't bat an eye over the fact that we were in a same sex relationship (that's what they are called in church). But even though I was incredibly happy, I was also being completely tormented in my head by the thought that I was sinning again, making Jesus unhappy, and therefore back on the road to Hell. Often when the thoughts would

48

torment me I would tell Itty "you are a sin." I would tell her that I was with her because I was weak, but one day we were going to have to break up so that I can get back right with God and marry a man. I told her that it was God's will for me to have a husband and that our relationship was sinful. Although I'm sure that was always painful and even offensive to hear, Itty just kept on loving me and going on and on about how I was her future wife. I would let myself get lost in thoughts of burning in Hell forever and fear would fill my whole body. But then I would look at her and fear would turn to love. Eventually I jdecided that if being with Itty, being this happy, finding belonging and a home inside this beautiful human being meant that I was going to burn in Hell forever, then I was just going to have to burn. Because this was love. This was God. It felt like communion around the dining room table. I wasn't letting it go.

One day I just prayed. I surrendered. I made up my mind and I prayed the way I had since I was a little girl. I just told God that I was sorry for still being gay. I told God that I knew it was a sin, but it really didn't feel like it. I told God how much I loved Itty. I also told God that I was going to stay with her even though she is a girl. As I cried, I told God that I had tried not to like her, but it didn't work; that I had tried not to be gay anymore, but it didn't work. I was in complete turmoil and so confused about what love was and what God was. Could this experience with Itty be it? No. The Bible said no. Even though my heart was saying yes. So I made a request. I told God that I was just going to have to live as gay because it wasn't going away. But I asked God to please just be kind and forgive me for it and to please just let me do this one sin because I couldn't help it, but please do not send me to Hell for it. Even in all the beauty I felt, I was still petrified of Hell. I begged God not to let me burn for eternity for this. I had tried and tried but the gayness wasn't going anywhere. I asked Jesus to just let me have this one and to please just let me go to Heaven anyway. I told God that I knew that this sin deserved Hell, but to please just let me into Heaven since I had tried. After that prayer, I was with Itty fully. I stopped calling her a sin. I stopped praying for a husband to rescue me from this lesbian relationship. I even called my mom and told her I was in love with Itty and that she was "the one." I came out to all my family members that I deemed "safe" and to all my friends. Hannah and I started making a habit of going "home" every so often for family dinner with Catherine and Louis. We were the real deal. We were a couple. I had finally found my way home. I finally belonged again.

FOREVER?

UARTS didn't offer student housing after freshman year, so we moved to a cute four-bedroom house in South Philly with two friends. Hannah and I had our own separate bedrooms, but we wouldn't dare actually spend a night apart. So my room really became "our room" and her room was more like a storage area and place she could escape to when she was mad at me.

My whole life I had been looking for something that would last forever. The devastating loss of Judy, of my family, of my stability, of my belonging traumatized me to a great extent. From the time I lost what I was deluded into thinking was true belonging with Judy, I began my quest for a place to belong forever. Once Itty and I were a couple I decided that this was it. This was my forever. I was very verbal about how we were going to love each other forever no matter what and I found great safety in that. Itty even bought me a necklace to match her Itty necklace, but mine was a heart and inside of the heart instead of it saying my name it said "Forever." I cherished the necklace but mostly I cherished the words. Finally, someone wanted me. I wasn't rejected anymore. I wasn't abandoned. I wasn't alone without my person. I replaced my longing for Judy (because no, it never went away) with a new person—one who would stay forever. A person who would not let me go. I was young then and wounded. I had no idea that that's what I was doing and no idea that it doesn't work that way. So when storms came, as they do in every relationship, I didn't speak to the storm and tell it to cease. I didn't sit in peace knowing that I was safe. I didn't wait for the storm to pass. I did the only thing I had ever learned to do: I freaked the fuck out. My greatest fear became losing Hannah. Any small disagreement or a change in her tone of voice sent me into a full-blown panic attack where I would kick and scream and cry the way I did when I was being taken away from Judy. In my mind it was the same thing (even though I didn't realize it at the time). I felt responsible for snitching on Bill and disclosing my abuse. I felt that because I did that, I lost Judy. In my eyes, it was a punishment. I had done something wrong and received the worst punishment imaginable for it. So now I was projecting all of that onto my relationship with Itty. Whenever I did something that upset Itty and she responded, I immediately went into full-blown panic—begging, pleading with her not to leave me and repeating how sorry I was. Now, this was of course irrational. She on the other hand would simply say something like "I am sorry, I see why that makes you uncomfortable. I won't do it again." And then get up and start cooking eggs or something, humming a Beatles song as she did it. This infuriated me. I was not used to this. For me, there had to be a fight. There had to be chaos. There had to be tears and pain. We couldn't simply express our feelings calmly, listen to each other, and then compromise on how to make ourselves feel safe in the relationship. I didn't even know what that was. So Hannah would be humming and cooking eggs in the kitchen after what to her was just a normal conversation, and inevitably, after just a matter of seconds I would erupt. Like a fucking volcano. The whole house would hear it. I would spew out the lava of rage coming from a feeling of extreme neglect and fear. I would be burning up all over. I would yell at her at the top of my lungs. I would force her to get upset. Force her to argue with me. Force her to feel pain like I was feeling pain. And then I would force her to promise never to leave me. Ever. Because we were in this forever, and I was sorry I got so mad and I loved her and she was my person and please don't be mad at me. It was a vicious cycle that just got worse with time. I needed the chaos. It was all I knew. The thing that had attracted me to her, her being a solid rock became the thing that I set out to destroy because I didn't feel safe with her being so solid. I needed her to join in on my drama, my storm, my chaos, my brokenness. I needed to smash her. She was my person, so I demanded that she share in my pain. And I would often say anything I could to make her feel pain. Because my pain was so lonely. I didn't want to be in it alone. This of course was dysfunctional, toxic and damaging. But it was all I knew. I was doing my best. I just didn't know any better.

Don't get me wrong, Itty was not perfect. She did some fucked up shit during our relationship that was deeply hurtful, and she was also dealing with her own anxiety, depression and rage. It takes two to tango. But this isn't her story, it's mine. So I am taking responsibility for my part in the story of us. I now see and acknowledge my part in the destructive patterns that were the destruction of "The Lesbians."

Mine and Itty's story of love and pain spanned over about five years: the entire time we were in college and then a year after. In the final years of "us" we would break up. We would date other people. But our hearts were still completely intertwined. Everything about Philly reminded me of her, of us. We had the same friends. I walked past the job we used to work at together every day knowing she was inside, my heart dropping down to my stomach feeling in such close proximity to her. I did not know how to live in Philly post us. And I didn't see a reason to. She really was my reason, and as we messily untangled ourselves and created more and more space between us, it just became painful to live in her city. Her city which had become our city and now was her city again. Without her, I felt like a misfit. I felt like a person without a home. Worse, I felt like a person who had lost her home, again. So I did the only thing I knew how to do: I fled. I fled to South Africa and threw myself fully into what I knew I loved: kids and the arts. I started a new life without Itty. The only way I knew how to get myself out of the mess that we had become, was to leave. There was a gap between me being so in love with her, the pain of losing her and me being okay again. But the thing that made me "okay again" was to do the same thing I had done with Itty with something else: to give myself fully to it. To fall in love with it and find my home there. Something else beautiful. So I fell in love with Africa. She was big. She was Black. And she was beautiful. I had been to Africa briefly before as a teenager, but now I was ready to dive into a deep long-term relationship with her. Before I tell you about our long-term relationship though, let me tell you how we met.

AFRICA

The show YEA is most known for is called *Soweto, Soweto, Soweto: A Township is Calling!* We performed this show several times a year. It was kind of like your rite of passage to YEA membership was learning, rehearsing and performing this show. Doing "Soweto" as we called it, was hard. It had been passed down to us from the older generation of YEA members who created it themselves and even performed it in South Africa at a festival in 2000. It was a show about the youth uprisings in 1976 in Soweto during apartheid. We all played South African youth rebelling against apartheid which was a system of institutionalized segregation and discrimination based on race in South Africa from 1948-1991. I played a young girl named Miriam whose house was being invaded by the soldiers and her family being taken away. As I said, there were no scripts in YEA. There was no sheet music. The script, music, lyrics and choreography lived inside of the older members who had created it, and inside of Freddie's and Charles's creative geniuses. So learning "Soweto" was a full body, mind and spirit experience. No one got to performance day without having sacrificed their fair share of blood, sweat and tears. As we absorbed the show into ourselves through transference from the older members and Freddie and Charles teaching us, our sacrificial blood, sweat and tears would drip down to the floor of Lang Carson. As we left the space I imagine that they mixed together and rose as an offering to our ancestors and those who actually did march in those uprisings and gave their lives for the right to be treated like human beings.

As young Black kids with our traumas from our lived lives, from those who raised us and those who came before us; as young Black kids living in America fighting for a space in the world—fighting to be seen as and treated as human; as young Black kids healing, hurting and being restored, "Soweto" was our battle cry. We tapped into the spirit of the youth of 1976. We tapped into the pain, but we also tapped into the joy. And that young Black joy made huge shifts within us and everyone who watched "Soweto." I also believe that that joy reverberated back through the generations and pleased those who were not able to access it in their own lives. Performing "Soweto" was experiencing the Divine. It was experiencing everything Freddie had taught us. Once we were on that stage and the djembe began to play and we began to march and open our mouths to the call and response that began the show, we were in another world— a world where pain was okay, where joy was okay, where "can't" did not exist, where our talents were fully displayed and we healed through them, where we felt connected to both our blackness and our Africaness and we let it express itself fully. It was a world where we moved to the beat of the drum that moved to the beat of our hearts, where there was no hierarchy, no person better or more important than another. We were an ensemble, brothers and sisters, family. Anything was possible and we were not afraid. During the whole show, no one ever left the stage once. The only instrument we had even as we sang complicated melodies and harmonies was the djembe. There was no set, no costume changes, no makeup. Just beautiful Black bodies with beating hearts existing, taking up space and creating something beautiful together.

The experience of "Soweto" changed my life for more reasons than one. Actually being a part of it was obviously a holy and life-changing experience, but it also lit a flame of desire in me to go to South Africa. We did so much research about these characters that we created and portrayed and about this place called Soweto that I became so curious about what the place was really like and was vocal about my desire to go there one day. Mystically, one day after rehearsal, my friend Marcus found a piece of paper on the floor of Lang Carson. He picked it up and read it. It was a flyer inviting young people to join an essay contest. The task was to write about a global leader that had created change in the world through peace. The prize was a two-week trip to South Africa to visit places like Soweto and Robben Island and learn about the way the Kingian philosophy of non-violence had helped lead to the end of apartheid. The opportunity sounded exciting, but with school, work and rehearsal, my teenage plate felt very full. So I put the flyer in my backpack with no intention of ever actually doing anything with it.

But then one day I was going through my backpack, and I found the flyer. I read it and saw that the contest was about to end. All essays had to be postmarked by the end of day the next day. As I stood with the piece of paper in my hands for just a moment something happened. It wasn't grand. It was quick and simple. I held the paper in my hand and soon I had a moment where I felt grounded and clear. I knew that I was supposed to write an essay and submit it, and that I would win. I knew I would actually achieve my dream of going to South Africa for the first time.

Now, the clock was ticking. I had to write the essay, edit it and submit it that same day in order for it to arrive in time for me to qualify. So without even thinking twice, I played hooky from school and wrote an essay about Nelson Mandela. This was not hard for me. Research was a big part of preparing for "Soweto." Freddie always encouraged us to learn as much as we could and use what we learned to create complex characters within the ensemble. So when researching a show centered around apartheid, we of course learned all we could about Nelson Mandela. I spilled as much of that knowledge as was necessary onto some pages, read it through once and made edits, printed it and then raced to submit it before the post office closed. I arrived at the post office huffing and puffing, put my essay into a large envelope and submitted it just in time for the deadline. A few months later I got the news that I had been selected and was going to South Africa! Most of the costs were covered, I just needed to pay an amount toward my plane ticket. I worked my ass off at my restaurant job to make as much of the money as I could. My dad also gifted me a large amount. From my paycheck I was also able to help one of the other girls who had been selected but was having a hard time coming up with the money. I got my passport in order and met the team. Before I knew it, I was on my very first international flight to a place that had existed only in my imagination. My whole outer and inner world was about to expand. I was about to meet people who talked differently than I did. I was about to see land more beautiful than I had ever seen before, meet real-life heroes and learn about peace and reconciliation. I was about to have my ignorance exposed for all to see, including me, in very public places; and to be exposed to poverty in a way that I had never experienced in America before. I was about to meet the risk-taker, rule breaker, natural leader that I had now become or maybe always had been. I got into a lot of trouble on this trip for breaking rules and challenging authority and mostly for following my curiosity to lead me into dangerous places we were told not to go. We were instructed to stay in the safety of our posh hotel at night. But after the experience of sneaking boys through Danielle's window, I knew a little bit about getting around rules like those. I remember sneaking out of the hotel one night to go to an area behind the hotel that we were specifically told not to go because it was dangerous. Naturally, that's exactly where I wanted to be. So I went one night. It was the first time I saw men holding sjambok—leather whips—in real life like we had mimed in "Soweto." This was also what I remember to be my first experience up close and personal with an area where sex workers lined the street corners. I had never gone to a place like this in the U.S. My privilege had shielded me from ever seeing the areas like this that exist there. Mixed in with the sex workers were the street kids sniffing glue and begging for money. I had never seen this before. Not because it doesn't exist in the U.S., but just because I had never been exposed to it. Seeing this was confusing because the South Africa I was experiencing with the group was so different. It was lush, green landscapes and super nice hotels and eating at fancy restaurants with amazing food. The adults even went shopping for gold jewelry one afternoon because it was cheaper there than in the U.S. I was experiencing this beautiful, high-end life during the day and then at night I saw the complete opposite. This was the first time I was confronted with the reality that South Africa is basically a first-world country and a third-world country at the same time. There are parts that are super fancy and developed and modern and beyond anything I could ever afford to experience in the U.S., but then there were areas of extreme poverty. The gap between the rich and the poor was *huge*. This confused me and caused a flame of curiosity and anger to begin to flicker in my chest. I wanted to understand. I wanted to know more. And I was angry. Poverty made me angry. Like I saw at the Red Shield, a fucked-up system (apartheid in this case) had again oppressed Black people and caused them homelessness and lack of basic needs. It tried to strip them of their dignity. This time in their own country. I was pissed about this. It was unjust. And I would not keep my mouth shut about it for the entire trip, even as we ate dinner in restaurants that gave you cloth napkins and served fancy fine dining versions of South African dishes inside walls that protected us from seeing the hungry outside. I was expected to smile and enjoy the experience I was privileged to have—and sometimes I did. But mostly, I would sit and try to reconcile being in such a nice place eating the way I was, knowing what impoverished Black South Africans had to do to feed their families in the townships that night. We were Black too. But we were here, and they were there. I just couldn't get over that. It wouldn't leave my mind. Even as I went back to America two weeks later, even as I moved to Philadelphia to go to UARTS a couple of months after, even as I fell in love with Itty, and especially not when I needed to run from her arms and back into the arms of Mother Africa.

I was only eighteen years old when I took that first trip to South Africa, and I hate to sound like a cliché, but basically I am one. On that trip to South Africa I felt drawn to and embraced by the country—the continent even. I knew I wanted to come back. I knew I wanted to do something about what I had seen. But it wasn't just about what I wanted to do for South Africa, it was also about what South Africa was doing for me. It woke me up to passions that I didn't know I had. It began to make clear the paths that had seemed dusty before. It embraced me. It gave me the opportunity to use my art as a gift to children to help them heal from systemic trauma. So when I knew I needed a place to land, new arms to fall into, that's where I returned. In 2010, after college, after Itty, I moved to Cape Town, South Africa. It was a move that would change the trajectory of my life forever. Once again, a Black mother, Mama Africa, was saving my life.

I must say Africa was not the only arms I was tempted to run into. I had trained to be an actor. I had spent years honing my craft and I was also tempted to deep dive into the opportunity of moving to New York—maybe even making it to Broadway! I wanted that. I wanted that deeply. I still do. New York was a woman of her own as well. She was sexy, fast-paced, creative, spontaneous, fun, wide open. I felt like I could run around freely inside of her the way Hannah and I had in the snow that night. I felt like I could be creative. That I could laugh hard and make great memories. I loved New York. I wanted New York. I wanted to move to New York and become an actress. But I had to choose. I couldn't have them both. And after some deep reflection and prayer I came to the decision that yes, I wanted New York and she was a valid and a totally acceptable choice. She would welcome me with open arms, and I would probably be successful and happy. But I felt that I needed Africa. She wouldn't just welcome me with open arms, she would draw me into her, press my head into her breast and remind me I was home. She would save me. She would draw out my deepest dreams—my destiny—and lovingly launch me into it. She would hold me as I wept from despair and pain that never went away and inspire a joy that only she could. She would tend to my soul. I needed that. She wouldn't allow my "success" to be only about my own happiness and fulfillment, but about collective happiness, freedom, creativity and peace. So I chose her.

CHAPTER 6

Traveling Girl

CAPE TOWN 2010

Before I traveled to Cape Town, South Africa all alone in 2010, I did what I thought was excellent preparation for my journey. On my previous trip to South Africa I had made a connection with a very nice man named Pastor Vusi of Crossroads Baptist Church. When I decided that I wanted to move to South Africa in 2010 I emailed him, and we began corresponding. He helped me plan my time in Cape Town. Most important, he introduced me to Sigcawu Primary School where I began corresponding with the principal and made a commitment to run a performing arts afterschool program for one year for the children in grade 7. After fundraising to sustain myself for the entire year I had found a place to stay that seemed nice and I was excited about (this was before the days of Airbnb). I had arranged transportation from the airport to the house and planned my trip so that I would arrive on Saturday and have time to rest before jumping into work at the school on Monday morning. The whole seventeen-hour long plane ride to South Africa I was over-the-moon excited. I remember being picked up at the airport in the darkness of night only to arrive at the house I had been so excited about and to find that the host had accidentally double booked my room that night. It was late. It was dark. I was in a new city, in a new country. I was surrounded by luggage, awash in expectation, and bombarded by disappointment and fear. And now to add to that, I didn't know where I was going to sleep that night. Nothing and no one was familiar. I felt lost and unsafe and alone. I was still young then—twenty-three years old. Eventually I found a temporary place to stay in the same neighborhood as the house I would eventually live in long term. I don't remember much about the temporary place. But what I do remember is when I finally laid my head on the pillow to sleep I released streams of tears. Where was I? What had I done? Did I really just uproot my life and move to another country where I knew no one and now was uncertain if any of the plans I had made would actually happen? Natasha and Danielle were not a phone call away. I felt so far from Itty. I remember not even knowing where the bathroom was to get tissue to blow my nose. I felt extremely alone and scared. It had all happened so fast. I had made a huge life decision that was so far outside of the norm. As I cried, I soothed myself by telling myself that I would move into the long-term house tomorrow, that the school was expecting me on Monday, and that if I was good at anything, I was good at making friends. So I would be fine. Then somehow I drifted off into the first night of sleep in my new city at the start of my new life.

LOVING HIM, LOVING HER

As I sit here, more than a decade after landing in Cape Town, reminiscing on my time there almost feels like a dream. It feels so long ago. Almost so long ago that maybe it didn't even happen. But it did. My memories of that time in my life are also filled with many emotions, from really good to really painful and some things in between. I'm also a person who likes to understand things, and when I am honest, I don't really understand what happened to me during the span of my life when Cape Town was home. But I know that it happened, and it was real. Then, it was so very real. Now, years later, after doing so much deconstructing of my faith, I look back and have a feeling of being unsure or lacking understanding of some of the most impactful experiences there. Or even the whole experience itself. But what I do know is that as it was happening it was absolutely real and I was very sure of it. I also know that it has changed me and changed my life for the better, absolutely, without a doubt.

The next day after waking up in my strange accommodation I did indeed move into what would be my new home for the next several months. It was lovely. The home was run by a woman who had the spirit of a butterfly, of glitter, of love, laughter and sensuality. The other people in the home were also travelers. Because I was there long term I met lots of people as they came and went. The home was in a neighborhood called Observatory. Very cute. Lots of bars and cafes within walking distance. I could walk to

59

the supermarket to do my shopping. The weather was usually good, or at least that's how I remember it. And that year the World Cup even happened in Cape Town. My friends and I made some of the best memories during World Cup 2010. So much football. So much cheering. Lots of dancing to the anthem. I didn't understand the game and wasn't even much interested in it. But I loved the feeling of getting together with all my friends and feeling the energy of excitement and playful competition. I loved jumping out of my seat and screaming with joy and crashing into my friends' hard hugs when "our team" scored. I loved having a reason to gather almost daily with the people who had become my new Cape Town family.

The thought that I had as I drifted off to sleep my first night in Cape Town was absolutely true. I made friends quickly and easily. Cape Town becoming home for me wasn't a process and didn't take any work or even patience on my part. I just kind of slipped into it like a hand into a glove. My best friend in Cape Town was (and still is) a beautiful woman named Mpho. We met when studying together at University of Cape Town during my senior year of college. Remember how I said that after my first trip, I knew that I wanted to be back? Well, I made it happen several times over the coming years. After that first trip I returned for a second time to study abroad for six months. To date, that was one of the happiest times of my life. So many wonderful experiences and great friendships came out of that trip, but the best by far was Mpho. We were fast friends, deep friends. Before I knew it we were spending every moment together. We spent our days attached at the hip going from class to class and eating lunch at our regular places. She would sleep over at my house, and we would spend the night cuddled together in my twin bed, our hearts embracing each other just as our bodies were. Mpho and I were not lovers. There was never anything sexual between us. But we were so much more than friends. The best word I can think of to describe our relationship is "soulmates." We love and accept each other from the depths of our souls. And we find home in each other. We find safety. We find a place to be truly and deeply ourselves. And then all that authenticity and vulnerability crashes into the other and is accepted with love, grace and warmth. I call her "my heart." Because that's what she is to me. And that's who she was during my time studying abroad and when I got back to Cape Town in 2010.

Besides Mpho and the World Cup, lots of other amazing things happened in Cape Town in 2010 as well. Somehow over the course of all of my World Cupping I met a group of Christians who welcomed me as a friend.

At that point in my life I was exploring spirituality in many different ways because although I could not comfortably find a place inside Christianity because of being gay, I still felt close to God. The Spirit's daily movement in my life and in my heart was undeniable. I am deeply spiritual, but at that time I didn't have a name for my practice, my belief system or my religion. I had released that when I told God I was going to be gay either way. But prayer and spiritual practice was a part of my daily life. And as much as I felt rejected by Christianity, I somehow managed to still be aware of God's embrace. Even as I explored spirituality in as many ways as I was exposed to it, I also still would sometimes go to church and was even a part of a small group of church members who met every week to pray and study the Bible together. I loved being a part of the community. I loved worshiping in church. I loved the positive messages that came from the sermons. But I was always careful. I kept my distance, knowing that as a gay person I was not completely welcome.

As time went on and as church people do, my friends from church began to show me more and more love. Before I knew it my small group and I had created a little family. We would go to one another's homes for dinners almost daily. We watched movies together; we went to football games together; we did coffees and drinks and braais (South African bar-b-ques); and we prayed together a lot. Eventually we all became so close that I felt I was being inauthentic by not coming clean about my sexuality. I felt like I was betraying myself and all the hard work I had done to come to accept and love who I was. I also felt like I was faking the friendship a bit. Who and how I love is a big part of who I am, so how can I call myself family to you when I am not only not telling you about this part of me, but actively hiding it out of fear of being rejected? I had done it enough in my youth and wasn't willing to do it anymore, so I decided to come out to my new church friends. 1

I had already come out to Mpho when I was studying abroad in Cape Town. She was the first African person that I had ever come out to, and I was scared shitless to do it. Being gay in America is one thing. Being gay in Africa is totally different. By the time I came out to Mpho we were already best friends who shared a bed daily and were very comfortable around each

---

1. I want to acknowledge that being able to live authentically and out loud like this is of course an advantage afforded to me by my privilege. Most people in South Africa, and in the world, are unable to do this even if they want to. It would put their very lives in danger as well as their basic needs like belonging, shelter, food, safety and other things they need to survive.

other, like sisters. I thought that after telling her she would be disgusted and offended. I couldn't have been more wrong. The night that I told her, life went on as usual. We talked about it. She had some questions. I answered them. And then we got tired and crawled into bed, cuddled, said goodnight and drifted off to sleep like any other night. Even though I was her first gay friend, it didn't faze Mpho at all. I don't even remember any shock in her response. It was just like any other new thing she was learning about me. It even made us closer because I was able to share with her about Itty and the pain I still felt from the breakup. She became a huge support for me in this.

But coming out to my church friends was different. Mpho's love was solid, unwavering, sure. These new friends were, well, new. And they were Christians. At this point Christian to me still meant anti-gay. And because we all went to church together I already knew my new friends' and our church's stance on homosexuality: it was not of God. It was something that needed to be prayed away in Jesus' name. A sin that needed to be overcome like lying or cheating or stealing. I had been here before. I knew how this went. So I prepared myself for a repeat of rejection by Jesus, the church and my new friends. I prepared myself to feel unworthy of saving and being kept safe. I prepared myself to be unworthy of the love of God.

When I came out to them I made it clear that this part of me was not something that was up for being changed. I made it clear that I am gay, and I have accepted that and embraced it and that it's a part of me and they had the choice whether to continue in friendship with me and accept it too, or to part ways with me and try to pray my gay away in private. I wasn't up for trying to be changed … again. Surprisingly, these new friends of mine reacted quite well. Their initial reactions were incredible: "We love you. We love all of you. And so does Jesus." I was shocked and undone. Wow. I was elated. Could this be true? Could God even be like this? Could God love and accept me, all of me? Not in spite of my gayness, but including it? I'd never considered it until that moment, through the love and acceptance of my small group. I felt like for the first time I got to keep my authenticity and the church and Jesus at the same time. These two parts of myself didn't have to war against each other anymore. Finally, I felt like I could have both.

The acceptance of those friends after coming out remains special to me. For most of them I was the first (openly) gay person they had ever met after having been taught for their whole lives how sinful, wrong and disgusting we are. But they chose the way of Jesus. They chose love. They reminded me that there is space at the table for us all. That I belong, I am welcome, I have a home in Him. I am worthy of a savior and a God. It felt amazing. This incredible display of love helped launch me into what I then called "getting saved, for real." This time I didn't just "accept Jesus into my heart" quietly and politely. I jumped into the embrace of Jesus, wrapped my arms and legs around Him like a small child does to a parent, buried my head into his chest, and held on tight like I never wanted to let go. I now call this period of my life my "Jesus freak" phase. This Jesus was less like my sister savior model in Tiff, and more like a squeaky-clean version of Grandma's Jesus. If there was ever a point in my life when I was the textbook definition of a Christian, it was during this time. What I was experiencing felt absolutely real and beautiful. It healed me in ways that nothing else ever has.

I had the sweetest love affair with Jesus at the time. I was all in. Head over heels in love. Jesus and His love felt tangible to me now. I would break down in tears of ecstasy and joy over this daily. I had found home again. I was so happy. So deeply happy. I drank Jesus like water in a desert. He was all I thought about, all I talked about, all I dreamed about, all I wanted. This was also when I got really into praise and worship. I absolutely loved closing my eyes, lifting my hands and worshiping Jesus with everything I had in me. He was "the pearl of great price" for me. He was worth giving up everything for. Jesus was all I wanted, all I needed. And I loved to tell him so through worship, dance, service to the poor and any other way I could. Still today, I love Jesus with my everything. Jesus and the love that is Christ is the one thing I am sure of even if I don't fully understand its workings. I didn't yet see that it was the same God incarnate in the sister-savior model and Grandma's Jesus. But I was slowly discovering this.

I was discovering the sacredness of incarnation. Being reminded that my first savior, my first Jesus, was a person. An incarnation of God. So this Jesus must be too. At the time that was pretty much the only way I thought about Jesus, but as I discovered and explored more over the years my beliefs about Him began to expand. I started putting the puzzle pieces together and realized that my little Black girl sister savior and Grandma's Jesus were the same. Incarnated differently. Both love me and want me to be free. Even as I began to deconstruct the image of father, son and Holy Spirit I felt tenderness as I replaced those images with my mother, my sister and the Holy Spirit that came over me at the altar at Grandma's church. The liquid love that made the other entities divine. I began to correlate divinity with Blackness, liberation and safety.

I am curious about all the people who lived before Jesus the man was born into the world, and I wonder with excitement about all the other ways God incarnated Himself and even "saved" them before coming down in a human body. I also wonder how God is still doing that today. How God is meeting us as nature, as forgiveness, as energy, as acceptance, as other people. I meet God often in the ocean. Each time I walk into the sea I can feel the Great Love so present, washing over me, healing me, saving me, meeting me again and again. My experience is this: God is as real to me now as He was when I understood Him based solely on the Bible and traditional Christianity. Sometimes I meet God when I wake up in my favorite little beach town in East Africa, opening my eyes to life again for another day and being awed by the wonder of that. Then of course walking into the Indian Ocean and immersing my body in the waters and sensing the presence of God which usually feels like a big breasted Black mother. And as I immerse myself with full abandon open and ready to meet Her again I hear Her saying, "Come on in baby. Good morning."

So how did I get from way down in South Africa to a beach town in East Africa? Well that my friend is nothing short of a miracle. It was a shift even I wasn't expecting. Warm your cup of coffee or tea. Or pour yourself another glass of wine. Get comfortable and I'll tell you all about it.

ELLIE

I cannot conclude the telling of the portion of my life in South Africa without mentioning the woman, the legend: Ellie. There are people who come into your life and mark it forever. That is Ellie for me. There are people who come into your life, flip you over, butter you up like a pancake and pour warm yummy maple syrup love all over you, which also changes you forever. That would also be Ellie. There are friendships that are for life. Friendships that challenge you, grow you, heal you and make you belly laugh without effort. That would also be my friendship with Ellie. There are people who birth little people into the world and give you the honor of being named their godmother, which gives you a whole new reason to keep living every day. That, my friends, would also be my Ellie.

Who is Ellie and how does she fit into this story? Put lightly, Ellie is my best friend. Put honestly, Ellie is my very own gift straight from God. She's my sister from another mister. She's my everything. I love her to the moon and back. When I introduce Ellie to people I usually say "This is Ellie. She's the one who brought me to Christ!" That was and is true. But now I see that it wasn't a one-time event. Ellie brings me to Christ every day. For me now, being born again isn't something that happens once and for all amen. I believe I am born again over and over. When I'm lucky, I find myself being born again daily.

But in the traditional sense of the word, Ellie is the one from my small group in Cape Town who officially got me "saved" when I came back to God, gayness and all. It happened amidst all the World Cup madness and friend making in Cape Town 2010. Ellie and I were fast friends. Sadly, this has nothing to do with me. Ellie is fast friends with everyone she meets. I have never met anyone who has met Ellie and doesn't consider her one of their really good friends. Ellie is an American girl born and raised in Detroit who inherited her mama's big heart. Put simply, Ellie is a lover. And she loves hard. We first met while studying abroad in Cape Town and experiencing the death of a close friend of hers while they were traveling the Garden route. That friend (Terrance) was a devout Christian. After they were both swept up by an unexpected wave that carried Terrance to death but spit Ellie out for another chance at life, she gave her life to Christ and became a devout Christian. She has never wavered ever since.

To my surprise, Ellie returned to Cape Town in 2010 for another semester after having her initial one cut short by Terrance's death. We saw each other, we hugged and we have basically been besties ever since. When Ellie came back she was on fire for Jesus and so was I. Naturally that became the center of most of our conversations and our friendship itself. But the big moment happened one day when we were taking a train to visit a friend who had recently given birth to twins. At that point I was almost all in with the being a Christian again thing, especially since my sexuality hadn't excluded me this time. But there still was one thing holding me back from jumping all into Christianity. It was the whole Hell thing. In our church/ denomination we were taught that anyone who does not become a Christian goes to Hell. That still didn't sit quite right with me. What about all the millions of people who practiced other religions devoutly and were genuinely good people? And I mean really, God is God, right? Certainly there could not be a hierarchy of gods. And if there was, of course we would all think our God is the "true God." Wouldn't everyone think that they are right? Isn't that human nature? If there really were lots of gods and only one was the "true" God, if there really were many religions and only one religion was the "right" one, how were we so sure that the true god was our

God and the right religion was our religion? And worse, how could we be so sure of this that we go so far as to say that if you worship any "other" god or are a part of any other religion, not only are you deathly wrong, but also when you die you will burn for eternity in a place called Hell? This seemed irrational and totally extreme, elitist and downright cruel to me. The way I see it, a person's religion is based on many things. Some things as simple as geography. As Christians, what we were saying was: Born in India to a Hindu family? You had no choice in this whatsoever; it was just the place, family and religion you were born into. Live there happily your whole life devoutly practicing your religion and moving through life just like the rest of us without ever randomly coming into contact with some (usually white) missionary who tells you about the one true God and leads you in the prayer for salvation which leads you to convert to Christianity? Well, too bad! Your fault! Burn in Hell forever! The end. You worshiped the wrong god. You were the wrong religion. That makes you a sinner worthy of eternal torture. Does anyone else find that whole thing really extreme and well, unfair? Even as I write this I feel the pang in the injustice of that stance in my heart. But this is what I was being taught to believe as a Christian. It was the thing holding me back from being all in. So on that train ride I decided to ask Ellie about it.

I voiced my deep concern to her about this stance as our train rattled along on its way to the town where our friend Lendy lived. It was a passionate and distressing conversation for me. I don't remember exactly what Ellie said, but I do remember the conviction in her voice, the absolute assuredness. And I do remember what happened after she said it. Using the example of the person born into Hinduism above, Ellie passionately explained to me that if that person never came into contact with Jesus and Christianity and therefore ended up in Hell, it was in fact not their fault at all. It was ours. *What?* She explained that as Christians it is our responsibility to go into our own communities and into all the world and preach the gospel of Jesus so that people can be saved. It was our responsibility to make sure that every person on the planet had a chance at salvation, an opportunity to meet Jesus and be saved from Hell forever. Instead of contemplating how unfair the situation is, my job as a Christian was to take action. To get off my ass and do all that I could to make sure that as many people as I could possibly reach came to know the good news of Jesus, accept Him into their hearts, convert to Christianity and be saved from Hell.

Okay, so this perspective wrecked me almost as much as the whole Hell thing itself did. You mean to tell me it's *my* fault as a Christian if people all over the world don't come to worship the "true God" and end up burning for eternity? Fuck! I took in what she said, considered it and somehow came to a place of acceptance of it. That was the last thing holding me back from committing every single piece of myself to Christianity. So once I accepted this last morsel of understanding about how Christianity works, I decided that I was all in. But if I was all in, that changed everything. It meant that my new mission in life needed to be not only to save people from harm like I had been saved all those years ago, but to save people from Hell by introducing them to the one true God, the Christian God. "*Okay*," I thought.

I began to talk a lot to our church friends group about the importance of us evangelizing so people could be saved from Hell. One day as I was talking to a friend of ours about this, he explained that a person who goes around the world evangelizing had a title in the church world. It's called being a "missionary." He also explained that I was actually already a missionary! He told me that the kind of work I did was exactly the kind of thing missionaries did. All I had to do now was add in the part where I evangelized to them. The formula: feed them, give them your service and then get them saved. "*Got it!*" I thought. So from then on, when I met with my kids after school in addition to allowing them to share their stories and create performances about them in an effort to use the power of storytelling and artistic expression to heal them, I also added in the part where they needed to accept Jesus or else they would burn in Hell forever. Unsurprisingly, this was not news to them. They lived in a colonized country in a township to which missionaries had been flooding for years. They all knew how this worked. I was actually the newbie here. So just like that my program became my mission, I started calling myself a missionary, and I felt like a good functioning Christian doing my part in the world to make sure we all ended up in Heaven with Jesus after we died.

MISSIONARY

My time as a missionary in South Africa is one of my fondest memories. It was marked by deep connection and laughter; by love and tears with the students I worked with—"my kids"; and by gatherings with my new church friends who had become family. We gathered a lot. Almost always around food. We sat around so many tables together like the disciples did in the

Gospels. I hosted weekly Sunday dinners. I cooked with so much love and shared all I had. My friend Natalie came and worked with me for six months. This precious time together has marked us for life and created a special bond that only we understand. We knew each other during the Sunday dinner in Cape Town days. During the Jesus Freak days. During the days where we drank both spiritual and physical wine in copious amounts daily.

By the time Natalie arrived I was a completely different Brittanie than the one she knew the last time we'd seen each other in the States and decided that it would be fun for her to come work with me during my time in Cape Town. Natalie knew "The Lesbians" Brittanie. She knew the Brittanie who helped people because it was the human thing to do, with no agenda of saving them from Hell. So when she arrived and met Missionary Brittanie, she was understandably shocked. But like a gust of wind, she too got swept up in the movement. She fit right into my new Jesus-freak-evangelizing-missionary life. And she fit right into my new family.

At the time, I was beginning to believe that my gayness was like the thorn in Paul's side (2 Corinthians 2:12). Paul is a character in the Bible who talks about a thorn in his side given to him by the devil. No matter how much he prays, God won't take away the thorn, which torments Paul. He says:

> I was given a thorn in my flesh, a messenger of Satan, to torment me. Three times I pleaded with the Lord to take it away from me. But he said to me, "My grace is sufficient for you, for my power is made perfect in weakness."

In my Christianese days I learned how to read the Bible in a way that told me what the church was telling me, regardless of what I was actually reading with my own eyes. The more I read it the more shame began to come back onto me like a slithering snake. I was in turmoil again. And the more time went on with my family of friends I became aware of their true stance on my gayness which was supported by our church and scripture. Their stance— which also became my stance—was: "Yes, Brittanie. We love you unconditionally, gay or not. And so does Jesus. You are welcome. You belong. You are not rejected." And at the same time, if I really loved Jesus I would be moved by love to obey Him by not give in to homosexual "urges" anymore. I could renounce my gayness and choose either a life of celibacy or a life married to the husband that God would bring me if I prayed for it. I was back to the same place I was when I met Hannah: gay and in pain because of it. Wanting so badly to be worthy of God's acceptance.

Eventually, I would join the ever-growing community of "ex-gays." Initially, I was so appalled by the thought of marriage to a man, I decided that I would live a life of celibacy and service. I decided that it would be best for me to be a missionary traveling the world evangelizing and bringing children to God, and who just also happened to be gay as fuck but was resisting it because: Jesus. At the time this felt like the best plan. But shockingly to all of us, mostly to myself, several months later I found myself in love with one of my best friends in Cape Town. And you guessed it! He was a man! This had to be Jesus. This had to be an answered prayer. This had to be a miracle! Oh my God, Jesus has brought me a husband after all! I am not going to be celibate forever! Yes, I am still very attracted to women, but I am head over heels for this man! My dream has come true! Let's start planning a wedding! And fast! Before I wake up and realize that … I was projecting a false fantasy onto him and using my relationship with him to prove to God, the world and myself that I could be a normal Christian girl. I really could join what was then called the "ex-gay" movement: people who have same sex attractions but have decided not to act on them. I mean, this guy was perfect. He was a leader in the church and like a big brother to all in our friend group. I remember he used to kiss me on my forehead when we embraced. I loved that. I have never met anyone who loved Jesus as much as he did. His heart was pure and beautiful. He was just genuinely a really great person. He was very handsome. And he was "safe." He was living a life of abstinence until marriage which we all believed was the only correct Christian way. He was just so Jesus-like in my eyes. I fell in love with the Jesus in him, and before I knew it I found myself physically attracted to him too. He had really dark skin. I loved watching him talk because the contrast between his black skin and his red tongue was gorgeous. When he asked me out, he basically told me that he had been praying and he had come to the awareness that God might be saying that I was his future wife. He asked me to take a few days and pray about if I wanted to begin a courtship with him which basically meant dating (without having sex of course) and with the intention of getting married. I melted. It was a fantasy come true. "*Oh my gosh,*" I thought. "*God will be so happy with me!*" I would fit in with my friends and family now because I was in a straight relationship, I thought. I am going to marry the most Christian guy ever and live a life that makes Jesus so happy instead of a life of sin with a woman, I thought. I am not going to Hell! I prayed about it for a few days already knowing the answer when he came to my house to hear what God had said in response. Yes!

Yes, I would court him. So from that moment we became an item. We were happy, we were in love, we were excited about the whole thing. So were our friends and our church. And so was Natalie. And Ellie. It was perfect.

JOSHUA

My relationship with Joshua was a whirlwind. Surprisingly, as I write this, I miss him. He was really good to me, and his intentions were pure. However, the pressure of him being "the one" and the little piece of truth that I didn't want to accept caused me to end our relationship after a couple of years. Most of our relationship was long distance. After we had been officially dating for six months or so, Joshua and I were in church one day. We were standing in one of the front rows worshiping (as we did). One of my hands held Joshua's while the other was raised to the heavens in worship. Eyes closed, tears falling, you know the scene by now. It was like a slideshow running across my vision. The racing images almost knocked the wind out of me. Floating, I squeezed Joshua's hand. Suddenly my eyes sprung open. I looked over at him. His eyes were soft; the eyes of a beautiful man whose heart was breaking. "I have to tell you something, babe," I said.

"I know," he said.

I didn't have to explain what I had seen; what God had shown me. "It's time for me to leave South Africa and go back to America," I said, a huge lump in my throat.

"I know," he said.

He pulled me into his arms, kissed my forehead and we embraced, my head on his chest, both of us weeping and hurting but fully surrendered and committed to whatever God said, even if it was, "Go back to America." We embraced. We worshiped. We surrendered. We said yes. And we kept doing that, whether geographically together or apart, until eventually the little anxious voice, the one deep inside me saying "this is not it" began to get louder and louder. In the beginning I could drown it out with worship music or hearing Joshua's voice. I could drown it out by repeating scripture over and over to myself. But after a while, what used to be like a baby's sweet cry became a full-blown toddler tantrum. Instead of admitting that this was coming from inside of me I totally projected it onto Joshua. I blamed him for not making enough money to care for us and our upcoming union. I blamed him for not coming to the States to meet my family and ask my dad for my hand in marriage fast enough. I blamed him for being comfortable serving the community right where he was instead of having a burning fire inside of him that blazed him into missionary life like me. I came up with a lot of reasons that at the time felt true and absolutely reasonable. But looking back, I think the reason I really broke up with Joshua was because that screaming toddler inside of me eventually learned to talk. She began to speak clearly. Soon, I was telling my friends, "I love Joshua, I really do. But not in the way I loved Hannah. I don't think I will ever be able to love him the way I love women. I will never love him the way he loves me." It wasn't fair, not to either of us. Before I knew it, I broke that beautiful man's heart. And I found myself alone again. Me and Jesus. Jesus ready to talk about the rainbow-colored elephant in the room. Me in total denial. I just insisted it was not there even though it was so big it was suffocating me.

MOZAMBIQUE

In 2012 I spent three months in Pemba, Mozambique at missionary school called Harvest School hosted by Iris Ministries, one of the largest and most esteemed missionary organizations in the world. It was one of the best times of my life and it propelled me into the beautiful life I have now. We spent hours each day basking in the love of God. Us. The straights. No other agenda. Just receiving God's love and in turn pouring our love back to Him. It was intimate. It was holy. It was fun. It was sacred. I lived in a tiny room with five other women, squeezed into bunk beds. The bathrooms were outside of the room; we shared them with tons of other girls. This is where I learned the art of the bucket bath and really thinking before flushing the toilet. "Wait, did I just poop or pee? Pee. Okay, no need to flush this time. Waste of water." Modern toilets and showers are definitely available in Mozambique—a beautiful country with incredible beaches where many people take luxurious vacations. But the mission thought it important to use the money made by the school on necessities like feeding us every day instead of fancy modern showers. I appreciated it. I would rather take a bucket bath than miss a delicious daily lunch of rice and beans. It's crazy to think about how bougie I have become. Nowadays, I would probably say something like "I can't eat beans every day because the gas hurts my stomach." Hilarious. In the Mozambique days I ate that plate of beans and rice for lunch every single day and did it happily. On good days I had access to some hot sauce or some seasoning salt that I added it to the beans. That changed the game completely. It was like a whole new meal. I remember being really nervous when I first got to the school and realized that all the other toilets except for the ones in our living area where pit latrines. I had used pit latrines many times before in South Africa. But to be honest, I had never pooped in one. I did not know how. The thought of squatting to poop and making sure I was positioned correctly in the dark latrine so that the poop actually went into the hole and not somewhere around it while also trying not to fall in, made me nervous. Using a pit latrine is not a big deal. Lots of people use them. But for my American self this was new, and I didn't know how to ask, "Hey, can someone teach me how to poop properly over a hole in the ground?" which basically translates to "I'm a bougie American who has used toilets my whole life and other fancy machines for simple everyday tasks. Because of this my brain and body are finding it difficult to figure out how to do something so simple and innate as pooping in a hole." I had too much pride to say that, so I figured it out by trial and error. The errors were not pleasant.

Life in Mozambique was very simple. The school intended it to be that way. It's scary to write about certain African countries because many people have an image of Africa shaped by Feed the Children commercials. When they hear "Africa" they tend to generalize. That may be tempting, but please don't. My experience of living in Mozambique was basic and simple because that's the way the school intended it to be and that was the best use of the money the school had. Not all Africans live this way. Not all Mozambicans live this way. Just look at a tourism magazine or reach out to someone who has been to Mozambique for perspective. This goes for all the other African countries I mention in this book as well, and for Africa (the continent) overall. This is a memoir, so it is about me and my experience. My experience is my own. It's based on choices I made for many different reasons like the amount of money I had at the time or what I intended to accomplish. The media has painted a picture of Africa for Americans that is very, well, white supremacist. It's degrading and untrue. These pictures of Africa are very problematic, and I want no part of adding to them. Africa is a diverse continent with diverse countries, cities and villages. Some of the most beautiful I have ever seen. I know in America we don't see that on TV or in books but I've seen it with my own eyes and by doing a quick Google search, you can too. In the meantime, here are some photos of me in some of the most beautiful places I have ever been on this continent, just to give you some perspective. Yes, on this continent I have taken many bucket baths and pooped in holes. I have also experienced the glory of the warm Indian ocean on clear sandy beaches, I have stayed in five-star hotels and luxurious villas with chefs to make our meals. I've shared bottles of delicious South African wine with friends on top of mountains while looking at the jaw-dropping view. What I am saying is, contrary to what we see in the media, Africa is beautiful, and Africa is diverse. Say it with me! Africa is beautiful and Africa is diverse. Great, glad we got that sorted out. Now off of my soapbox and back to the story.

DURING MY TIME IN MOZAMBIQUE God healed a lot of the wounds I had from the sexual abuse in my childhood. Healing is an ongoing journey, but the depths of healing I experienced at Harvest School—usually while lying on my back with my palms open to receive, totally focused on the heart of Jesus—was significant. Those old feelings and memories of the abuse re-emerging and bringing them to the heart of Jesus and my community made space for compassion and empathy in me. I began to feel compassion for young girls who were being sexually abused. I had visions of them during the day, I dreamt about them in my sleep. My heart was constantly heavy with the knowledge that there were many young girls who were in so much pain because they were being sexually violated and exploited by men. The heaviness weighed on my heart, but I didn't let it stop there. I continually brought all the pain and all the heaviness back to the safest place I knew: the heart of Jesus. Over and over. And my community. I remember that I would close my eyes and visualize Jesus' heart: love itself. It looked like a prism of rainbow-colored light. All different colors of light shining from a source of immense power. It was so beautiful. I still often hide myself there when I need to. So moment by moment I would bring the burden I was now carrying daily of the awareness of the many girls all over the world whose innocence and whose bodies were being violated back to the heart of Jesus. But then I was reminded that bringing this pain to the heart of Jesus wasn't enough. Like my prayer in the bathroom when Bill was molesting me, my prayers were not enough. Just like Black women had come and rescued me, liberated me, kept me safe, I needed to step out and do the same for these girls. I needed to be a sister savior. My liberation was bound up in theirs. I had to do this for all of us.

So when a young woman came to our school and shared about the issue of child sex slavery on the Kenyan coast, girls as young as eight years old having to sell their bodies for basic needs like food, clean water, or the cost of school, my heart wasn't just heavy, it was completely split open, and my life changed forever.

Most mornings the thing that wakes me up and gets me out of bed is the feeling of having to pee. Well one morning in Mozambique during the missionary-Jesus-freak days, I woke up and as I opened my eyes, before I could even realize that I had to pee I just heard the word "Kenya" in my spirit. I know this sounds strange. That's because it is. It wasn't an audible voice. It felt like it came from inside of me. But it was crystal clear: "Kenya."

"*That's weird,*" I thought and continued on to the bathroom. When I finished peeing and got up to pull my gray pajama bottoms back up, I looked down and saw that the tag on my bottoms said, "Made in KENYA." But the word Kenya was huge and when I read it my heart started to burn like fire. Again, this sounds strange. Because it is. But as I am learning and accepting more and more, I am strange. God is strange. Strange can be beautiful.

I left the bathroom and hurried back to my room and told my "house mom" that I thought God was telling me to go to Kenya. I knew there was an outreach trip planned for Kenya. I told her that I really wanted to join that team, that I needed to go to Kenya. She tried her best to get me on that trip, but serendipitously, it was totally full. There was no space for me. "*Okay,*" I thought. I figured maybe I had heard wrong. I let go of the whole "random" Kenya idea and continued on with life at Iris. At the time I had my life all planned out. I was going to continue to enjoy every minute of every day of time at Harvest School, then I would take a short break in South Africa to visit Josh (that's when the breakup happened) and then I would get on a plane to Cameroon to start my new life as a missionary at an orphanage there. I had agreed to run the orphanage as the previous person had left and they were looking for someone to take over. My plane tickets were already purchased, dates in the calendar were already marked. I knew each step of the way for my life moving forward. Or so I thought. I was excited for my new life as a celibate (secretly gay) single missionary in some west African country I had never been to and mothering a ton of kids in an orphanage whose name I can't even remember right now. At the time it seemed like the most Christian thing to do. It seemed like it would make Jesus happy. Just the sound of it: "*Single-celibate-missionary who gave up her life of American comfort to live in a village in west Africa and run an orphanage.*" At the time, that sounded really Jesus-like to me. I thought Jesus was all about sacrifice and giving things up for him like he sacrificed and gave his life up for us. Because I loved him, I was eager to do the same. So I got dressed and ready for class that day intending to forget about Kenya and move on with my plans. But when I got to class there was this skinny blonde woman there at the front. She had come to speak to us about her life as a missionary in the Congo and yes, you guessed it: Kenya. She had been visiting the Kenyan coast for a few years and was horrified by the situation of child sex slavery there. She even had a plan to open up a rescue home for young girls who were trapped in this situation of exploitation. It would be called Bella House. A home for girls to heal and be provided with safety, love and all their other basic needs and more without having to sell their small bodies to big men. And of course, most important, they would learn about the love of Jesus and learn that it's because Jesus loved them so much that they had been rescued from their pain by missionaries and brought to a place of safety and love. My eyes closed. We went into worship, and I had The Vision:

I was inside the heart of Jesus. Jesus asked if I wanted to go into His favorite room. I said yes. He opened the door, and it was filled with kids. Extremely happy kids playing, jumping rope, blowing bubbles, playing hopscotch, laughing. As soon as the kids saw Jesus walk in the door they screamed with joy and hugged his neck and jumped all over him, pulling him to come play with them. They also greeted me and pulled me to come play. The joy in the room was tangible. It was an intense joy like I've never felt before. It was a free joy. It brought tears to my eyes. We played with the children for a while and then Jesus looked at me and asked, "Do you want to stay in this room with me?" I laughed at the question because I found it ridiculous. The joy I was feeling was the greatest I'd ever known. Of course I wanted to stay. So I smiled. "Yes," I said. We continued to play with the kids playing chase and hand games and having the time of our lives. Then Jesus looked at me again this time with a little sorrow in His eyes which confused me. He asked me again, "Do you want to stay in this room with me?" I replied desperately "*Yes!*" We played with the kids more, laughing and having a great time. Then Jesus turned to me with tears in His eyes and asked me a third time: "Are you sure you want to stay in this room with me?" I felt compassion and solidarity as I replied for the third time "*Yes!*" Immediately I was turned to the other side of the room.

It scared me. It was pitch black and completely void of joy. Jesus walked me over there. At the entrance there was a set of keys. He picked them up. We walked into the room. The darkness was so heavy you almost had to crawl. The atmosphere was thick with sadness and injustice. It made me nauseous. My first instinct was to try to find the exit. We walked deeper inside and came to a wall. The wall was as high and as wide as you could see. As we got closer I realized the wall was lined with cages. And as we got even closer I realized there were little girls in each cage. They were scared and they looked like they had been in the cages for a long time. I got close to one and the girl immediately shuffled to the back of her cage in fear. But then Jesus stood beside me and she was no longer afraid. Jesus put the key in my hand, and I put the key inside the lock and then my hand turned into the key. I unlocked that first cage and as soon as the girl stepped out of the cage she came out completely restored to her dignity, all cleaned up, absolutely beautiful and confident and she began dancing with Jesus. I kept unlocking cages and each time the same thing would happen: the girl would come out looking free, dignified and happy as she danced with Jesus. Then I heard: "I'm calling you to bring slaves into freedom." I opened my eyes and heard "Mama Heidi," the leader of Iris, speaking into a microphone: "We need people who are willing to give their lives to see the child sex trade in Kenya ended!"

Strange.

I pretty much couldn't talk for the rest of the day. I was in a state of shock. I'd had many visions in my life, some of which I do believe came from the Divine as a message, but I had never experienced anything as powerful and as real to me as The Vision. Something had happened. I didn't know what, but it was intense. All I could do was oscillate between crying, sitting in silence, or lying prostrate on the ground. I do remember Mama Heidi coming over and embracing me during The Vision and praying over me to be released into the nations to free many girls trapped in the child sex trade. She held me like a mama holds her child. We wept as she prayed over me with passion, fire and love.

Not long after that I got an email from my contact in Cameroon explaining that the orphanage was closing and basically telling me not to come. I got to South Africa and visited Josh the day Harvest School ended. We went from him giving me roses at the airport and kisses on the forehead to us breaking up that same evening. It happened within an hour of me arriving at his apartment. Before I knew it, I was using $300 of the only $400 I had to buy myself a one-way ticket to Kenya. "*I really hope I like it there,*" I thought "*because I have no money to leave!*" I laugh at that now of course, but as I sat on that plane bound for Kenya for the first time, writing in my multi-colored journal that my friend Yvette had given me as a going away gift months ago, I had no idea what was about to happen to me.

I had no idea that I was actually on a plane "home" for the first time.

CHAPTER 7

Kenyan Girl

ARRIVING IN KENYA was much different than arriving in South Africa. I had no plans, no idea where I would be living, only one contact and $100. But I must say, I also arrived with no fear and a deep sense of anticipation. I flew into the heat of Mombasa, got off the plane, grabbed my luggage and walked out of the arrivals door, my eyes searching for a skinny blonde woman whom I had only met for maybe five minutes in Mozambique. She wasn't hard to spot among the crowd of mostly stout male Kenyan taxi drivers waiting at arrivals for passengers in need of a ride. She smiled a very welcoming smile and embraced me in a hug. Standing next to her was a very joyful middle aged Kenyan man whom I came to know as Pastor. He smiled that big smile of his that I would come to know very well and excitedly said "Karibu!" He shook my hand in greeting and reached out to help me with my luggage as he explained that "karibu" means "welcome" in Swahili. "Thank you! Thank you!" I said excitedly. We walked out into the hot Mombasa sun to his van in the parking area and began our journey. Pastor rolled down the windows. My new friend and host, who I learned had grown up wanting to be a missionary in Africa, pulled down her sunglasses from the top of her head to over her eyes. We drove along in the van from Mombasa to a small coastal town called Mtwapa which would become my new home. Over the next few days lots of things happened. I got to know my new missionary friend more. We'll call her Julie. She taught me all she could about life in Mtwapa. She introduced me to where I could eat, where I could shop and where I could sleep. She put me on my first *boda boda* (motorcycle taxi). And she answered my many questions. She welcomed me into her simple yet beautiful life in Mtwapa, and so did Pastor. The first time Julie took me to Pastor's church I was welcomed warmly. There were lots of smiles, *"karibus"* and sounds of celebration. Julie and Pastor made me feel welcomed and safe. They made sure I felt like I belonged and was wanted. They quickly began to feel like family and before I knew it I was hopping on *boda bodas* all by myself, running errands or grabbing lunch in this new town. My transition to Mtwapa was easy and quick. I didn't have to strive for anything. It felt like I was exactly where I was supposed to be.

After a short adjustment period Julie began to tell me more about her dream for Bella House. My heart would swell whenever we spoke about it. She told me that she had already found the actual home and paid a deposit. Eeek! All that was left to do was wait for the official move-in date, fix the place up with mosquito netting and the other necessities, and then there was the final thing: to find girls to live there. This all sounded like exciting work. I was eager to help.

As we waited for the official move-in date for Bella House to come, two big things happened. First, she took me to take a look at the house. I still remember Pastor driving us in his van through the gates for the first time and me seeing the big white house. It was beautiful. Surrounded by grass and a gazebo as well as a balcony and veranda. The grates on the windows looked like hearts. I was in love. We walked inside and I oohed and aahed at the gorgeous spacious home. We went upstairs. Julie showed me the big room with the balcony that would be her room and then the extra smaller rooms for staff. I was already imagining myself living there. But then came the best part: the kids' room. She opened the door to a huge room lined with empty bunk beds. It was spacious with lots of windows for air and sunlight. It was a kid's dream room. Even the en-suite bathroom was huge. I immediately began to envision girls crawling into their cute little bunk beds and us being there to kiss them goodnight. *"Yes, this is it!"* I thought. And that's when I told Julie that I thought I wanted not only to help her start the home, but to live there and work as a missionary with the girls. Julie, being as welcoming and open as she was, responded with an easy "karibu!" There was lots of space in the house. I could even have one of the bedrooms. "Our girls" (as we began to call them before we even knew them) needed as much love as possible. So I was welcome.

Over the next few weeks we spent our time running lots of errands like going to buy paint and meeting with carpenters who could make furniture for us. Pastor would pick us up in the mornings in his van, me having had my coffee and Julie having had her tea. We'd climb in, ready for our day of errands to prep Bella House for our girls. Julie always made a point to insist that I sit in the front seat every other day which I thought was so humble, kind and admirable. It's something I learned from her that I try to practice today. It was a simple gesture that said: "you are welcome, you belong, there is no hierarchy, take the front." Before long Julie and I moved into Bella House, just the two of us as we continued to make it livable for the girls and set out to find them. I remember our days looking a lot like this at the time: wake up, do house-visits to girls Julie had already started building relationships with knowing they were stuck in the prison of having to sell their small bodies for basic needs, then head to the local supermarket called Tusky's to grab our routine cheap meal of premade what they called "Chinese rice" for lunch. We ate it pretty much every day because it was filling, and it cost the equivalent of one dollar. We would then go home and decompress from the heavy morning by eating our Chinese rice in front of her computer while watching reruns of *Friends* episodes. After hearing rape stories all morning, food and laughter was just what we needed. After lunch break we usually did admin work or other things that needed to get done. Once per week in the afternoons we went to Pastor's church, sharing one *boda boda*, whizzing through the village the church was in, to hold a program for girls involved in child labor. Julie had begun this program way before I arrived, so I just slipped in to help. Those afternoons were lots of fun because we did art and fun activities with the girls. I did drama games with them, and Julie was her bundle of bubbly love, dispensing free warm hugs and discipleship about the love of Jesus. We sang songs together in Swahili and danced the walls of the church down. And then, like clock-work, after every meeting girls would come up to us, first to Julie because they knew and trusted her, and then to me as they got to know me more. They came to us in confidence and shared their burdens. They told us about how difficult their lives were, how hard it was to live and function while hungry, and the even harder things they had to do to feed their hunger and the hunger of their families. I took my cues from Julie. The first few weeks I watched her listen to the girls with such attention, love and empathy. She made space for their pain and expressed her sorrow over it. And then I watched her each time hold their pain and their hands and bring both back to Jesus. Julie's love for Jesus was indescribable. She would pray with and for these girls with intimacy, compassion and fire. Her fiery love for both Jesus and the girl whose hand she was holding was obvious through her teary intimate prayers for Jesus to come in and save like he does. To make the wrong things right for this child. And most of all, for this child to experience the love of Jesus anew, like never before. I watched Julie, and I learned. It was like a formula that eventually seeped into my bones.

1. Make yourself available.

2. Genuinely smile at the girl as she comes to you to make her feel safe and welcome.

3. Listen with insistent compassion and openness, make space for her story, for her pain, don't be afraid of it, don't rush her out of it; hold space and listen with an open heart.

4. Express to her your deep sadness over the injustice she is experiencing and allow for compassion and empathy to flow.

5. Bring her and her pain back to Jesus. Always back to Jesus.

But I would soon learn again that bringing suffering to Jesus' heart wasn't enough. These girls needed to reach their arms out to the girls next to them and save each other. They needed saving and safety. They needed sister saviors.

OUTREACH IN MTWAPA

Time escapes me now, so I can't remember if it was weeks or months that passed when we found ourselves all moved into Bella House and ready to receive girls. I also can't remember at exactly what point Joy moved in with us. I do remember us interviewing Joy at our favorite cheap, simple, little cafe over *kahawa* and chai. We were in search of a live-in house mom who could care for the girls primarily, and also give them counseling. I remember Julie looking down at Joy's resume and smiling as she asked her about her counseling qualifications. Joy was very sweet and humble. She was also quite beautiful and very smart. I don't think we even interviewed anyone else before Julie offered Joy the job. And before long, Joy moved into Bella. And that's when we started our search for girls and continued with Julie's outreach to sex workers on the streets of Mtwapa.

Now, this is the part of the story that gets sticky. I cannot speak for Julie, so I will only speak for myself. At the time, my intentions were absolutely pure. I also fully believed what I had been taught in church and at Harvest School about what it meant to be a missionary. Simply: I had the good news of Jesus to share, and I needed to share it with those in "darkness." God is love. Whatever I did to my sister I did to Him. It was my job to "set the captives free," "feed the hungry," "clothe the naked." While these things could be noble and kind, the connection I had learned to make between these acts of service and sharing the gospel was problematic. I didn't see it then, but I see it now. Even as I write this I feel shame in criticizing the actions of my younger adult missionary self, because I truly felt like I was doing the work of God. It came from a pure place. But I had many blind spots at the time. It didn't even occur to me how problematic it was that out of 300+ students attending a school in Mozambique that sent missionaries to the "darkest nations on earth"—many being in Africa—only four of us were Black. By far, by a whole lot, the student population was white. All of us had been called by God to this school to prepare to be sent out to preach the gospel and save people from Hell, to feed the sick and clothe the naked. But not once did the question cross my mind: "Why are over 95 percent of the people called by God from all over the world to come to this missionary school white?" It didn't cross my mind. Not even once. I'm embarrassed to say, yes. I was that blind. So once Julie and I started doing outreach to "prostitutes" as we proudly touted them in our language and even in descriptions on social media and blog posts, I was blind to the power dynamics at play. I could not see how my believing that I carried the truth, the good news of Jesus that will save a person from Hell, made no room for the woman's experience or even her voice at all. My job was to preach, to teach, to tell, to lead to salvation. There was no room for these women, these "prostitutes" to correct me, disagree with me or even put me in my twenty-something-year-old place. Their job was to listen, agree and change. Even women who were older than me or had more life experience than me. Their job was to listen. I learned this at Harvest School. We did outreach there; it was one of the highlights of the school experience. But outreach meant hundreds of people, Mozambicans, coming and sitting in a large crowd. Then we, the missionaries (some of whom were Mozambican by the way but had been trained by our white leader and mama bear) would show them a film called *The Jesus Film*. The film was translated into their language, but the characters, yes even Jesus, especially Jesus, were white as fucking snow. Many would be touched by the story of Jesus. After they watched the film we would preach to them. I remember watching Mama Heidi preach to a sea of Black faces with such fire and love, so genuine, so kind. She would preach about this Jesus that we all were hungry for. This

Jesus that even now makes my heart melt, especially when I think of Mama Heidi describing him, Love Himself. But just minutes before we had seen a depiction of this Jesus in *The Jesus Film*, so although she never gave him a race or an eye color or any physical features, the sea of Black people, some of whom had never heard of Jesus before, already had an association of Jesus being the white man on the big screen. By this time I was so dissociated that I didn't even notice. These were the epitome of my Jesus freak years. The squeaky-clean Jesus. I still couldn't see the savior of my youth in this savior. This savior was better. Whiter. Cleaner. And very straight.

AFTER THE FILM, our Mama or another missionary preached about how amazing He was and gave these people a taste of His love that they would want to feast on forever. When a missionary would ask, "Who wants Jesus to come into your hearts tonight?" every single arm in the sea of people would rise, almost in unison. And they would all give their lives to Jesus. As I watched and listened, I was moved and found myself laying my heart before Jesus all over again. It was like liquid love. It felt so right. So honest. Even amidst all the problems. I now know that God can get glory in any place. After the preaching, people would come up to be prayed for and miracles would happen. I still don't quite understand this. But somehow, after introducing a sea of Black people, of Africans, to Jesus by a film depicting him as a white man, Mama Heidi would call for the blind to come up to the front. She would pray for them, and most times, the blind would see. It was a miracle. But we missionaries were blind to the white supremacy we were perpetuating. And because of the power dynamics of white supremacy, not one of those hundreds of people who came to our outreaches ever stood up and said no. "No, thank you. I don't want your white Jesus." Not one of them even stood up and asked why Love didn't look like them, but instead looked like the white missionaries all standing ready to minister to them. Because of the power structure (which was completely unintentional, but sadly, still absolutely wrong), there was no space made for them to do so. We had the mic. We were the teachers. They were there to listen. There was no Q&A. There was no request for feedback. There was no time to question. We were right. We had Jesus and Jesus was the only true way. So, every time at outreach after watching the film, seeing white Jesus, and then hearing how this Jesus was love and could save them, the sea of beautiful Black bodies all raised their hands in response to "who wants Jesus?" And they would convert to Christianity. They did the exact same thing I did in Dee's church the evening I destroyed my rainbow bracelet to follow God.

We would feed them and fellowship with them and crawl back into the tents in which we slept during outreach, feeling amazed and grateful that we had the opportunity to see so many people be saved from Hell and fall in love with Love. Well, that's what I felt at least. And that's what my friends expressed that they felt as well. So we kept doing it and devoted our lives to doing it. This was the model I also used when doing outreach to sex workers on the streets of Mtwapa. I preached to them with fire and love, telling them of the radical and unconditional love of Jesus that would bring them salvation. I didn't see salvation then as liberation and safety in this world. I saw it as a pass into Heaven in the next. So I asked them if they wanted this Jesus, if they wanted heaven. They said yes. We prayed. We rejoiced. And then we fed them. Julie and I would then hop on a *boda boda* bound for home, for Bella House. We would say goodnight to each other. And then I would crawl into my bed feeling the same way I felt when I crawled into my tent at outreach. I would feel *"Brittanie, you did good. You did a really good thing tonight."* And I would imagine Jesus smiling down at me, pleased, as I drifted off to sleep.

THE GIRLS COME HOME

Before long, we began to take girls into Bella House. We would still do our outreaches to sex workers on the street, but our main focus began to be identifying girls to bring into Bella. Before long we had six girls living with us: four younger ones and two older ones. The oldest was actually a young woman. I believe she was about eighteen years old at the time. She had been a victim of sex trafficking in Nairobi. Her story was heartbreaking and totally unjust, so although we had committed to working with young girls, we agreed that taking her in was the right thing to do. We had plenty of space after all. The other older girl we'll call "S." She was a feisty one. She didn't even agree to move into Bella right away. She liked her freedom. But after some convincing she came home with us. Then there were the younger four. Each girl's story was different and dynamic, and also her own to tell. So as tempting as it is to share their stories in an effort to further explain why making Kenya home and why "starting a family" for me was messy, unconventional and definitely not what my parents had in mind, out of re- spect for each of my daughters I will not do that. They are now all teenagers or young adults and are fully capable of sharing their stories if they want; every part: the good, the really good, the bad, the really bad. They have experienced enough exploitation, and I will not exploit them further in this book. So, let me continue to share what is mine to share instead: my own story, my own experience, even in becoming their mom.

'MAMA'

By the time all six girls were moved in, Julie was not in Mtwapa. She had gone back home to Canada for some time. Joy and I, along with another missionary who had recently arrived from Harvest School, were living in the house with the girls. I remember Julie being so sad that she couldn't be there to see the girls move in, but she had plans to split her time between Congo and Kenya so we all were happy to know that she would be in Bella with us as often as she could. In the meantime Joy, "Kate" (the new missionary) and I set off trying to run Bella. The plan had always been for Pastor's wife, Gladys, to be the house manager. Official Bella staff would be Gladys and Joy; and we even considered hiring a cook at some point. But according to my memory, as time went on, Gladys just never showed up. Eventually Julie had a conversation with her and Pastor to identify why she never stepped into her role. But while they were talking, I was working and so was Joy. We decided as a team not to hire a cook since Joy offered to do the cooking as a part of her mom role. She jumped right in as House Mom. Meanwhile, I slipped into the role of House Manager the way you slip into a perfect sized dress. It was natural, it was comfortable. It was necessary. I was there, Gladys was not. The work had to be done. So I did it.

Eventually Julie and I had a conversation where we officially appointed me House Manager and Bella House began to run like a well-oiled machine. I took care of all the administrative and operational things: the everyday management of the house; supporting Joy in her role as House Mother; managing finances; communicating with Julie and her financial director about receipts and money flow; the overall functioning of the house; nurturing the girls; facilitating daily leisure, recreational and educational activities; and assisting with cooking and everyday care for the girls. I was busy, very busy, but I was also very happy. To this day, my days at Bella House when things were good, are some of the best days of my life.

It wasn't all rosy, of course. There were lots of hard times. The work was hard, but because I had chosen this work knowing it would be hard, I was still able to find lots of joy in it. Yes, even joy in suffering. One of the hardest parts about trying to care for the girls in the beginning was that we did not speak the same language. I had not done the work of learning Swahili yet, so in those early days I remember sitting around the breakfast table eating our normal breakfast of bread with Blue Band and Kenyan Tea and feeling like such an outsider as the girls and Joy had conversation. They were bonding and getting to know one another. I could not understand anything they were saying. I felt left out, I had so much FOMO. The girls and I laugh about it now because many mornings I would even get so frustrated and sad about this that I would cry actual tears. I ached to get to know the girls, but not being able to communicate verbally felt like a huge hurdle that in the beginning felt insurmountable. I began to feel afraid that I would be this separate from the girls and lonely for a very long time. You see during those beginning days and weeks and months, Bella was my whole life. I did not ever take a break or have any interaction with anyone outside of Bella (besides via Facebook). I had basically martyred myself for the cause out of love, devotion and obedience to Jesus. At least that's what I thought it was at the time. Not bonding with the girls was especially painful because they were the only people around (besides Joy) to bond with. I had also had an image in my head of what it would be like to have girls in the house before they actually came. I had images of happy girls running around the house laughing and having fun as I watched and giggled with a smile on my face. I had a picture of what evening family time would like where the girls would openly communicate to Joy and me about how they were feeling and how the transition was going for them. I had a picture in my head of hugs in the mornings and goodnight kisses from sleepy girls with bed hair. I basically had a picture of the family I wanted and never had. Or was it a family I saw on TV? Or was it an image I learned from the church? I am not quite sure how this picture of the "perfect family" came into my head. But it was there. So when the picture in my head didn't immediately match what we had at Bella (mostly simply because of the communication barrier between me and the girls), I felt anxious to fast forward past this part, because surely in time the picture would come.

I wasn't entirely wrong about this. I learned two major lessons during that time. You can't fast forward past the time in a new relationship that is needed to create a foundation of genuine trust. You just can't. Especially with children who have experienced trauma. You may have anxiety to push the fast forward button, but there is no fast forward button. The foundation of trust and love that my relationship with the girls is now built on took time. It took tears. It took lots of awkward moments, rejection and misunderstandings. Amidst it all, I just kept showing up. Every morning I would wake up and show up. Eventually they began to see me as "the one who always shows up." I did a lot of hard things during that time trying to earn the girl's love and trust while also running the house. Showing up was the easiest of them all. My showing up every day wasn't even really something I was consciously doing for the girls; it was more of a choice that I made every morning when I woke up with the Holy Spirit. It wasn't hard to do. I guess I saw Mommie do it, show up no matter what. And now I was doing the same. Every morning I would wake up with a new determination to get up and walk down those stairs and show up for my new family. I felt like doing it every single day. So I did. Little did I know, the simple act of showing up was the greatest communication of love I was showing to the girls. In all my striving, trying so many different ways to communicate with them and bond with them and make moments with them, little worked. Mostly because that's simply not what they were looking for. They were kids at the time. They weren't looking for someone to do things right for them, not entirely at least. Yes, cooking their eggs the right way was important. But even more important, after being separated from their families and hurt by perpetrators, they were looking for someone who would simply show up every day. A constant. Someone they could count on to be there. And through all the highs and lows, through the language barriers and my own feelings of loneliness, through learning how to cook their eggs the way they like them and learning who liked kisses and who didn't, no matter what, every day I showed up. I woke up, walked down those stairs, and showed up for them. I didn't know at the time that that's what mamas do. Mamas simply show up for their children. I didn't realize it was the Mommie in me. Mommie showed up for me, so I showed up for them. Reaching across to liberate others who were unsafe and victimized the way Mommie had reached back and liberated me. Being rescued by a Black woman, then reaching forward and rescuing someone else.

Before long, in the girls eyes and hearts my role shifted. I went from being the Black American who ran the house and couldn't speak Swahili to being "Mama." First "Mama Brittanie," then simply "Mama." As time went on I became "Mom," "Mummy" or even "Mathe." I became the one they could always count on to show up. And before long my days and nights were filled with cuddles and hugs and kisses from them. I learned some of their language and they learned more of mine. Evening family time became an actual thing. We had inside jokes and learned one another's personalities. They knew that even though I shared tea with them every morning, I actually loved coffee. I learned each of their favorite colors, who liked dresses and who preferred jeans. And finally, after waking up with the Holy Spirit and walking down the Bella House stairs and seeing the girls seated around the big black table, I learned to say "*Habari asabuhi*" and was greeted with big smiles on mostly small faces with bed hair replying "*nzuri*."

SEPARATION

Time moved on at Beautiful House. The girls eventually started going to school after an extended period of staying at home with Mama Joy and me. We developed a routine that included weekly outings on Saturdays. Visitors, including Kate, came and went. I started taking Swahili lessons, the TV show *Scandal* came out during this time, so I learned how to access it all the way in Mtwapa which made me very happy. Joy began to take Sundays off, so on Sundays I would stay at home with girls and cook the meals and get them ready for the upcoming school week. For dinner I usually made spaghetti and tomato sauce. They hated every bite of it. To this very day they still complain about it.

A lot of the girls' trauma also began to surface at this time. So Joy and I, along with whatever volunteer may be around at the time, did our best to pray and support them through it. The girls also missed their families a lot, but for safety Julie (with our input welcomed and honored as equal team members) decided it was best if they stayed separated or had supervised visits. This is because in the stories that the girls had told us about their past abuse, their guardian usually didn't keep them safe and in some cases allowed or facilitated the abuse. This was a very sore issue for us at the time. We all felt so much compassion for the girls because they clearly missed their families, but we were trying to do what we believed was the best thing: keeping them safe and away from opportunities of re-victimization by keeping them at Bella.

The hardest part was mealtimes. In the early days I remember girls crying or choking back tears at the table. For a long time I did not understand why they would get so sad at mealtimes. The language barrier and lack of a foundation of trust in the beginning didn't allow for them to open up to me and be vulnerable about what was going on in their hearts. With time and Mama Joy's help, I learned that the girls would get upset at meal-time because we would serve them up big plates of delicious and nutritious meals three times a day without fail. We thought this would make them happy. But sometimes, in particular our youngest, would look at her plate piled high with rice and pojo bought and prepared with love and money, and her face would get red hot and she would bow her head, distraught, as tears began to flow. Sometimes she would even refuse to eat. I later learned that this was because of an intense feeling of guilt. It was hard for her to eat as much as she wanted whenever she wanted, to have access to a guaranteed three meals per day when her family was struggling for the money to have one meal a day. It broke her heart. Understandably so. And seeing food piled high in front of her just brought back memories and images of her family suffering from hunger. Many of the other girls went through a similar struggle. Finally, one day they were able to share their pain with me. I listened and together we came up with a solution. I decided to begin delivering food to the girls' families weekly to give them the peace of mind that came with knowing their mothers, grandmothers and siblings were eating every day and doing okay even without them being there. Before I committed to delivering food to the families, I knew very little about the girls' families aside from what was translated to me through a third party. What I thought I knew was that the girls were safer, removed from abusive situations and able to satisfy basic needs when away from their families. But soon my weekly food drop-offs turned into weekly visits that turned into weekly conversations that turned into budding friendships. These friendships were also based on the trust that came from me simply showing up, consistently, every week. I'd just sit with them, using my broken Swahili to listen to them and update them on how well their children were doing. I got to know the adults as well as the girls' siblings. I saw the care in their families and their love for one another. I saw their family dynamics, smiling and laughing together as their new toddlers took their first wobbly steps, crying together over how hard daily life was when living in poverty. For once, I was the student, not the teacher. This was what I now understand to be true outreach. I did not preach anything to them, not even the gospel. I listened. I did not take their agency away or their choice-making. I made space for them and their expressions and what they had to say. I took correction. I took a lot of correction. I learned to become a sister to them instead of coming in and pouring white saviorism everywhere. I was learning that white saviorism (which I was perpetuating), is hyper focused on having the power to save someone else, taking their agency away and pouring out benevolence on those who have less power than you. Then you feel good about it and probably post it on social media. That's totally different from being a sister savior. The ground on which sister saviorhood stands is that I am not free until you are free. We're in this together. It's not charity, but solidarity. I learned this from my girls' mothers and grandmothers. They helped me get back to sister saviorhood after my Jesus-freak missionary days. It's like they hit me on the head with a stick and said, "Girl, you are Black! You are like us. Sit your ass down somewhere." So I did.

DEBRA

In an effort to be transparent and not make a people group all good here, I must admit that not every family was the same. Of course it was more complex than that. But I would have never known had I not sat my Black ass down. While yes, most of the mothers pleasantly surprised me, others were exactly what we were told they were or even worse. Like one of the girls' mothers whom we will call Debra. She was a single mom raising her teenage daughter who eventually came to live with us at Bella, thank God. I don't know much about Debra's childhood or what got her to where she was when we met. But I assume she must have gone through a lot of pain. More pain than I can even understand. So much pain that she needed to cause her daughter pain just to cope. Debra was an alcoholic and always physically sick. I watched her body deteriorate before my eyes over the years. She just kept getting skinnier and skinnier. Debra was also angry. Deeply and incredibly angry. Her fits of rage would turn into violence toward whoever was in her path, which usually was her daughter. Debra and her daughter lived in a tiny room in Mtwapa and shared a bed. They said they loved each other, but Debra's daughter also inherited Debra's rage. They would fight verbally, physically, emotionally and psychologically. And they fought a lot. As Debra was the parent, this turned into abuse of every kind toward her child. There were many times that neighbors told me about how Debra would physically, in a fit of rage, fight her daughter outside their home for all in the tiny community to see. Her daughter would do anything she could to be at home as little as possible. She would escape to friends' houses or to nightlife of Mtwapa, even while underage. I remember being at a club in Mtwapa once undercover with our team looking for underage girls engaging in sex work whom we could rescue and bring into Bella. I remember seeing her daughter there with a much older man laughing and drinking. My heart broke and I was also disgusted by this older man taking advantage of this obviously much younger and more vulnerable child. Disgusting. I waited for a moment when she would be away from the man so I could jump in and talk her into coming home with us. According to my memory, there was a point where she got up to go to the bathroom. Joy and I were seated at a table near the bathroom, so we got up to talk to her. We tried our best to convince her to leave that man and come home with us instead that night. We tried to convince her to leave this nightlife altogether and come be with us where she can get an education and not have to engage in any sex work or sexual exploitation. But she was hesitant. She refused our offer and decided to stay that night with the man. I can only imagine the things he did to her that night. I never asked for details.

Debra's daughter's desire for love and acceptance from her mother despite the abuse made it difficult for her to want to leave her. Like many victims of child abuse, we tend to be in love with our abusers and want their affection and attention. Even to the point that we sometimes become addicted to the abuse because it is associated with feelings of what we think are love and connection with our abusers. This was the case with Debra's daughter. It was a longer road with her than it was with the other girls. While the other mothers practically begged us to take their girls to Bella House and the girls did anything they could to get the coveted slot at Bella, Debra's daughter was different. She was afraid of leaving her mom and she was afraid of losing her freedom. She was a girl who got high on the nightlife. It was also a means for her to cope with her pain. She didn't want to lose that. But in the end, Debra wanted her gone. This rejection hurt her daughter deeply, but she would do anything her mom asked of her. She loved her so much. And she was addicted to their lifestyle. Soon I began to hear stories that just got worse and worse about the things Debra was doing to her daughter. We were told that she was pimping her out and even using rape as a form of punishment for bad behavior. The fights were continuing, and neighbors were becoming more and more concerned as they watched the punches being thrown. Debra would often call us, complaining that she could not take care of her daughter, that their situation was desperate. She would beg us to remove her child from her home. It seemed like things were just getting worse and worse. The stories became so alarming that we moved to action and took her daughter out. The grotesque nature of the kind of abuse we were told her daughter was experiencing is more than

I care to repeat in this book. However, I knew that if what was going on in that home was what I think was going on in that home, I am grateful that we were able to take her daughter out. I only wish we were able to do it more quickly. We still don't have proof of what happened in that house, but what her daughter told us was sufficient. I had a conviction then that I still have now: if a child tells you they are being abused, believe them. So we moved forward from a place of believing her. I learned something as a tiny girl who told Judy that Daddy had abused me and she didn't believe me and told me I made it up in a dream. I learned that it's absolutely not my job to decide if a victim is telling me the truth or not. Taking on that job and failing the way Judy did can be fatal. My job is always to believe a child when they tell me they are being abused. Just believe. And then let the proper people handle the investigation. So I believed Debra's daughter, who has become our daughter. And I still do. And now as I work as a team with Debra to parent our daughter, I have happily taken on the role of being the mom who will not throw our daughter away no matter what. Even as she rages, even as she misbehaves, I will never give up on her and I will never throw her out. Like Mommie did for me. Like God does for us. I will keep showing up. I don't know why I have been given the grace to be able to do this, but I have. And I do not judge Debra for not having the capacity to do the same. She can do things for our daughter that I never can, like share memories of her childhood before I ever came into the picture or speak to her in a deep way using her mother tongue that makes the words pierce straight through to her heart.

I am now to report that after many years, Debra is recovering from her alcoholism and fixing her life. I can never be that example for our daughter of what it's like to be such a strong woman and make the resolve to pull yourself out of addiction and destruction with no formal help, only your own will, and come out on the other end stronger and better. Only Debra can do that. Only Debra has done that. Addiction and trauma make love messy and sometimes even impossible. But healing is always available. After many dark and painful years, I am grateful that in Debra and our daughter's story, healing is making itself known and clearing pathways for love more and more every day.

JULIE RETURNS

But now let's go back to the beginning of Bella, before I woke up. Eventually, after her furlough, Julie began to make trips to Kenya to live out her dream at Bella. It had been a long journey for her. The rest of us showed up after most of the hard pioneering work had been done. But for Julie it was different. Bella House was her dream baby. She dreamed it up, did the work to make the dream a reality and fundraised to keep the place running. Even during her furlough or when she was busy working on her projects in Congo she was sure to send money for everything we needed for the house and the girls every month. She would also include a salary for Joy. I worked as a missionary (volunteer) at Bella House. After all of the hard work, prayer and pioneering—all the emotional and energetic labor she put into Bella—I loved getting to see how excited she was to see her dream come true. It was so admirable to me. In one of her posts after coming to Bella for the first time after we had taken the girls in, she asked in awe, "Is this really my life? The other missionaries and myself just had this talk. *What?* We literally get to go into brothels, find the worst situations and rescue them into our beautiful family." Her dream, one she had since she was ten years old, was unfolding before her very eyes. I was honored to be a part of it.

To be honest, Bella was never my dream. It was always hers, and I was there serving. When I was ten, I did not see myself rescuing anyone. "Child prostitutes" (as we ignorantly called them during my time at Bella) were the furthest thing from my mind. When I was ten I was writing songs and making up dance routines. I was writing little plays and performing them for my family. My sister and cousins and I were busy creating talent shows and forcing the adults to watch them. It's been a long time since I was ten years old, but my memories do not include dreams of becoming a missionary, especially since I didn't even know what a missionary was. I'm not really sure what I dreamed of becoming. But I do remember creating, rehearsing and performing a lot. I don't know what I dreamed of being at ten, but what I already was at ten was an artist. Dreams of "rescuing child prostitutes" and even the use of such language came after "getting saved" in South Africa in 2010 and being introduced to "missionary work." That dream (and the use of that language) became amplified and defined through visions and experiences I had under Mama Heidi and all the other missionaries that came along to teach us at Harvest School. And so when Julie came along with her vision for Bella House, I jumped in as an actor in the script she had been working on with her Jesus since she was ten. We were both living out who we were since we were ten years old—her making her dream come true of being a missionary in Africa, rescuing child prostitutes and bringing them home to Bella and to the heart of God; and me doing what I had been doing since I was ten: performing my role to the best of my ability. But soon a problem arose in this scenario. After a while, it became clear that Julie was not only unhappy with the role I was playing, but also about how well I was playing it. I think I began to take up too much space in her dream. This was neither the first time nor the last time I would be shamed for taking up too much space or asked to be smaller. This issue came to the forefront when the girls began referring to Julie as "auntie" instead of what we all expected them to call her: "Mama Julie." The girls referred to Joy and me as "Mama Joy" and "Mama Brittanie" so naturally we assumed that they would refer to Julie the same way, but they did not. Understandably, this was painful to her, and she expressed that to us. We tried to fix it. We spoke to the girls and invited them to call Julie "mama" as well. The two older girls made the shift easily, but the younger ones did not. We explained to them that Julie loved them just as much as Mama Joy and I did, and her absence was not because of lack of love but because she was out there working to fundraise enough money to keep the house running as well as helping other children in need in Congo. But the younger girls were resistant to calling Julie "mama" and on top of that they began to bond with me and attach to me in a deeper way than any of us expected. Julie was hurt by this. Naively back then, I attributed the girls' refusal only to the fact that I just kept showing up daily and that's what they craved at the time. That's what they understood the role of a "mama" to be. But now, years later, they still talk with shock that I expected them to call a white woman "mama." It didn't feel right to them.

Julie was hurt. This was her dream. Her home. Her organization. Her labor of love. She had birthed this. After a while, something that was never there between Julie and me began to creep into our relationship: tension. Julie went from being someone I looked up to—my role model, dear friend, mentor and leader—to being something else. Something that felt threatening to me at the time, something that felt hurtful. I think she began to feel the same way about me. This happened slowly because we both valued and loved each other, and because we shared such a deep love for the girls. So we fought for our connection, our friendship, our being on the same team. But what began as a low simmer of tension began to grow and grow the more time Julie spent at Bella with Joy, the girls, Kate (who was also there at the time), and me. I probably should have seen this coming, but my worship of Julie blinded me to it. She was blonde and white and pure. She loved the squeaky-clean Jesus. She was also straight. She was what I was supposed to be. I remember once in the early days when it was just the two of us living together in a big empty white house eating Chinese rice from Tusky's together every day for lunch she said something that shocked and confused me. I immediately tried to dismiss it because it would pop the bubble of the dream we were living. So I turned what felt like a tiny stab into a compliment. She said to me as we were at the checkout counter paying our 100 shillings each for our Chinese rice lunch, "You know, at first when we met, I saw you walk out of that airport, I never thought we would be close friends. I am so happy I was wrong."

I wondered, *"What about how I looked walking out of an airport made you immediately judge me as a person you would not have a close friendship with?"* But I quickly silenced that thought, because she was perfect. Instead I decided to gush at the fact that this woman whom I admired so much for her genuine love of Jesus and the way she lived it out actually liked and even loved me and considered me a dear friend. I chose to be grateful for that, to praise Jesus for it and to push my initial reaction deep down somewhere far away, expecting never to remember it again. We were sisters, or so I thought.

THE EXODUS AND BURNING OF DREAMS

Not long after the tension began, it rose to a point where Julie asked me to leave Bella House. She told me that I needed healing, basically that I was too broken to be "in the field" and needed to go get some "inner healing." It began with her asking me to leave temporarily, but after experiencing my reaction and the reaction of the girls to such a ludicrous and belittling request, she decided to change her request: now she was asking me to leave for good. Needless to say, the girls were not having this, and neither was I. She was trying to separate us in hopes of breaking what she saw as an unhealthy bond. My bond with the girls was not and is not unhealthy. It's just pretty divine which can be scary to someone who isn't in on it. It can make them feel excluded. In confidence, I had opened up to Julie about my sexual abuse and my history of what felt like Judy's abandonment. I shared this with Julie as a friend in confidence. I told her that working through these things with the girls was bringing up my own past memories of wounds that I was still on the path to healing. After the tension came to a boil, she used this against me. She said that I needed to heal these things before I could effectively heal others. I had to be perfect and clean in order to liberate. Like White Jesus was.

Let's be real. Healing is not linear. It is an ongoing process. There is always room for more. It's not a destination, it's a journey that invites us deeper and deeper into its warmth with every trigger, every open conversation, every action taken to come closer. To be fully healed before I could continue mothering the girls was absurd. That's not how it works. I don't believe that any amount of what she referred to as "inner healing" (which is a kind of Christian counseling) could ever get me to the point of being a Brittanie that was never hurt. No amount of Jesus would erase what happened to me. If anything, my experience of sexual abuse and abandonment—being a healer who was healing—made me more qualified to mother the girls, not less. The kind of Christianity that we learned from white evangelism (what Julie was operating from) places a huge emphasis on purity, being made clean, being fully restored. Healing even physically means that your sickness completely goes away with strong faith and prayer, often in an instant with no process. There is no space for the God who came back with holes in his hands and feet. The scared Jesus. And especially not the Jesus who was God incarnate in a Black girl body. No. This Jesus was white and holy. We rejoiced and praised God when a person who was blind instantly could see after we would pray for them. Healing wasn't a process, it was instant. Instant and complete healing was the only kind of healing that Jesus was interested in. And we would teach that person to give a testimony pretty much like this: "I once was blind, but now I see." I reject that narrative now. I reject the narrative that there is no gray area in God. I reject that God has only worked in my life if I am no longer who I used to be. I believe God wants us to carry all parts of ourselves into our stories. And that's what I was doing.

I once was a victim and now I am a survivor. Yes, I have been through years of therapy and done years of healing work, but I will never proclaim that I have arrived at the destination of healing as a place where there is no room for more. I am still the Brittanie who was abused. I still love her. I will not amputate her from myself. I reject the idea that healing must have reached a final destination for you to be healed. I believe that God is still God if I am blind, even if I still don't see after prayer. That God is still God if I get partial sight after prayer. That God is still God if I am blind and happy to be blind because: fuck ableism. God is not only God when my darkness, my history and those old parts of me completely disappear. I don't have to be whole for God to be God. I believe in the *enoughness* of God's grace. Where I am is enough,

When I was working with the girls in Bella then, I *was healed and I was healing.* Julie wanted my story to be something complete and clean that we put up on our blogs and social media pages. Even I did it. I started being ashamed of parts of myself and only showed the whitest parts. I was also stuck in that toxic narrative demanded by white saviorism. She wanted my story to be that once I was broken, Jesus put me together and made me whole. The end. But that was not and is not my story. I am what I am and that is enough. What God has done in me is enough. All my parts. Even my gray. Especially my Black. I love how Sarah Bessey says it: "I am still sick and I am healed and I am always being born again over and over." My healing and my salvation doesn't end. It keeps going. This was my truth then and that is my truth now.

Julie wanted me to be a Brittanie who had never been hurt. A half Brittanie. I couldn't do it. So she used that as a reason to add onto the list of reasons that I was unfit to be at Bella parenting the girls. When she told Joy and the girls that she was asking me to leave and that they would instead stay at Bella with her and Joy for now and then she would bring in new parents for them, their response was a quick "no." Joy refused to continue working at Bella after hearing Julie say such a thing, and the girls refused to continue living there as well. The two older girls decided to stay and to her delight, accepted her request to call her "mama." But without Joy, the small girls and me, the house crumbled. We had become Bella. Our family made Bella House what it was. So although Julie's organization tried its best to make use of the gorgeous home after we all left, the project crumpled a year after our exodus and Bella House no longer exists.

There is a popular song that is based on a passage from the book of Ruth in the Bible: "Where you go I go, where you stay I stay, where you move I move, I will follow you . . . . " After Julie told the girls that Mama Brittanie would be leaving, they began to sing it. "Where you go I go, where you stay I stay …" And that's what they did. Julie allowed them to leave Bella but didn't release them to me. They were told to leave all their material perks behind. Surprisingly, none of this persuaded them to stay. They had come to Bella for love, and this did not feel like love to them. After being released back to their families, they eventually came and found me. We were family again along with their biological families. And we still are today.

During their exodus is when I saw it. They bound together in sisterhood. Held onto each other tight and they chose freedom. They freed themselves and each other. They were each other's sister saviors. That was when the white savior suit I'd been walking around in began to wear out. They didn't reach out to the white woman to save them. They didn't even reach out to me or to Joy. They reached for their own divinity inside of their small Black bodies and set themselves free, holding hands as they leaped to liberation. As my white savior suit grew thin, I felt a little bit of grief that I had to come all the way to Kenya to remember what Tiffanie had taught me that night at the bathroom door almost thirty years earlier. No white savior is actually going to save us. Our Black ass sisters are. Reach across.

CHAPTER 8

Abolitionist Girl

ONE ALTERNATIVE TO SAVIORISM is what author and activist bell hooks calls a love ethic.

After all the trauma post Bella House, I needed a break. So I took some time away. I went to the States for a while, but first I went to Cameroon on an invitation from a Black woman named Sheri, who unknowingly was being a sister savior to me. Sheri ran a spiritual school there. I went to be a student and to be revived. When I got there I totally needed saving. I was completely broken. My heart ached. It was the gestures from Black women, sister saviors in Cameroon, that kept me alive. I felt like I was on the verge of death. Without them I would not have survived. Little did I know, this was my first major depressive episode. One of many to come. In Cameroon, I was at my lowest point. But something good came out of the bad.

When I left evangelism I left white Jesus, but I never left worship. One evening I was at church worshiping. It was a worshiping event where all we did was worship God all evening. I was worshiping and praying. Same story. Eyes closed. Hands raised. Tears streaming down my face. I was asking God what to do next. I knew I was going to go back to Kenya and continue raising the girls, but I wanted this to be different. I didn't want to create my own Bella. That wasn't my dream. I wanted to create something that came from me and my own giftings. I told God that I was struggling because I still had a heart for abolishing child sex slavery, but I also really still had a heart for the arts. That I didn't know how to do both, but I wanted to. The prayer felt like the prayer I had prayed years ago telling God I wanted Heaven, but I wanted Hannah too. That's when I heard the phrase "Art and Abolition." I heard it from deep within my spirit and as soon as I heard it I loved it.

The next day I got some markers and colored paper and sat on the veranda to create. I came up with the initial idea for Art and Abolition which was to sponsor the girls for school as well as provide art therapy camps for them three times throughout the year. I had so much fun planning what the camps would look like and all the healing modalities they would entail. I planned to have a mix of art therapy, art itself as therapy, and also psychotherapy at the camps. I wanted to create a space for the girls to begin the journey of healing from their pasts. But I wanted to do it in a way that was true to me: through art.

A few months later I went to the States and told Natalie all about my new dream. She was on board and wanted to help. How amazing! This was turning into something. This time *my* dream was being birthed. What happened next changed the course of my life. Natalie introduced me to Rozz.

In comes Rozz, one of the most bad ass, go-getter, visionary Black women I have ever met. I went to her house one day to meet her. Her baby twins were napping upstairs. I told her about myself and my past with Bella and my dream for Art and Abolition. She replied, "We are going to make this happen for you."

And she did.

To make this dream come true we needed to start a non-profit. She gathered about sixteen other women (mostly Black, mostly artists) and they became the founding board of the non-profit that we named "Art and Abolition". Together, operating out of a deep sense of sisterhood we were birthing a dream. We decided that six girls weren't enough. We were going to get even more girls in our program and put them in school and through our arts camps. I wouldn't be where I am today without the women on my founding board. They really launched Art and Abolition and fundraised the first big chunk of money to get us started through a Kickstarter campaign. By the time I was heading back home to Kenya to reunite with the girls, I had the sisterhood of all these new women, money to support us, and a new dream ready to blossom.

I ran Art and Abolition in Kenya for ten years.

I haven't always actually done the true work of abolition even as the executive director and founder of Art and Abolition. I entered the role still partly wearing my white savior suit. Turns out I was the one in the most bondage, the one who actually needed saving. I needed saving from the white Jesus *and* from white saviorism. I needed to remember who God really was.

I am grateful that when I knew better though, I did better. bell hooks calls the alternative to saviorism the "love ethic." This began to seep into my bones as time went by. As I was busy trying to be the best soldier in white Jesus' army the girls were busy loving and sistering one another. They were teaching me all along.

I think it was 2016 when I became obsessed with Harriet Tubman. She took me on an exploration of what the word "abolition" means. It all started when I was worshiping in a church in Brooklyn, New York. Her spirit kept coming to me. I remember writing this experience down. It continued during the active years of running Art and Abolition when Mama Harriet challenged my understanding of what that word actually means and invited me into doing the work of acknowledging and doing away with the remnants of my own white savior suit and stepping into what is the interconnected work of abolition and sister saviorhood.

It looked like the roadmap Mama Harriet laid out for us; it looked like what the girls, my little Harriets, were already doing: *I'm getting free and taking someone with me, and they're getting free and taking someone with them.* It looked like rejoicing in the fact that White Jesus isn't coming to make us white as snow after all. That we are Black. That we are glorious.

LITTLE HARRIETS

At the height of the Covid 19 pandemic I found a collage one of my daughters had made in her free time while cleaning the house. She had written "Our Family Values" in one section of the collage. I was touched. I excitedly looked at the section to see what she had written under that title. And that's when I saw it. It said: "Just because you help us doesn't mean you own us." I was gutted. But in the best of ways. There she was teaching me the lesson I was trying to learn the whole time. It was a sentence I wish I could have said to Bill and Judy as a child. It was like my daughter was talking directly to the lineages of white saviors who have tried to save us and saying a big "Hell no!" Their story was similar to mine. White Jesus never showed up for them. But their black ass sisters did.

CHAPTER 9

Bye, Girl

I DID ATTEMPT to go back to church when I returned to Kenya. I began going to a church led by a local pastor. I hated every minute of it, but I would make myself go. The service was long, the views were super conservative and I found myself bored. Eventually I decided to be kind to myself and stop going to a church I hated going to. I was still learning how to rebuild my relationship with God without my white savior suit anyway. So It felt right to stop oppressing myself.

I also started dropping back into myself in different ways from the time when I returned to Kenya and started A&A. It was significant because I was reunited with a community I deeply missed. The gays. I started going out with friends and living life again. We would go to live music concerts and art shows and restaurants. Nothing like my life in Mtwapa. We also hung out a lot at a place called Pawa254 known for its "artivism." Before I knew it, I'd found my tribe again. I went to my first arts event at Pawa254 with my friend Allison who was visiting from the States. When I opened the door all I saw were queers. My heart leapt before I could stop it. I was home. We walked in the room and there they were: beautiful, bold, Black and queer. That's when I told Allison my story and she introduced me to gay Christian spaces like Level Ground and The Gay Christian Network. I had never heard of this. I started reading about gay Christians and learning what that was. Finally, a theology that included my God and my queerness. Allison didn't know this, but the night before she arrived in Kenya I was actually on my bathroom floor crying out to God. Telling God again that I was still gay and begging again to just be myself like I did years ago.

That night I got some comfort as I felt the Holy Spirit bring me peace after I prayed. I felt that God was showing me that God is affirming of who I am. I began to reconcile my faith with my sexuality. Finally not running from one or the other. I started slowly crawling back to both together. It felt amazing. I got to bring all of me to life's table.